ECONOMIC DEVELOPMENT IN AFRICA IN THE AGE OF GLOBALIZATION AND HIV/AIDS

AuthorHouse™
1663 Liberty Drive, Suite 200
Bloomington, IN 47403
www.authorhouse.com
Phone: 1-800-839-8640

First published by AuthorHouse 1/10/2008

ISBN: 978-1-4343-5561-4 (sc)

Printed in the United States of America
Bloomington, Indiana

This book is printed on acid-free paper.

ECONOMIC DEVELOPMENT IN AFRICA IN THE AGE OF GLOBALIZATION AND HIV/AIDS

DANIEL K. SONG'ONY

authorHOUSE®

ABOUT THE AUTHOR

Daniel Kipkemei Song'ony is a professor of Economics at MidAmerica Nazarene University in Olathe, Kansas. He received his a BA from Trinity College, a MA from Roosevelt University and a MA and PhD from the New School. He has been on the faculty at the University of Nairobi, Trinity International University and the State University of New York. His main research interests are african economic development, poverty alleviation, globalization, political economy, gender and inequality in education and socioeconomic impact of HIV/AIDS in the african diaspora.

Dedication

To my wife, Nanette, who has helped me throughout
the writing of this book and making changes and editing.

Contents

List of Tables

List of Figures

INTRODUCTION

Purpose

The purpose of this book is to explain the determinants of poverty as it pertains to the largest resource of GNP in sub—Saharan Africa: the agricultural sector. As a case study, this book will investigate the relationship between agricultural exports and the alleviation of poverty in Kenya.

The causes of poverty are reasons for persistent underdevelopment in the whole region of Sub—Saharan Africa. This study shows that the structural characteristics inherent in Kenya can be generalized for the whole of Africa, south of the Sahara.

From the early days of independence, Kenya identified its enemies as disease, illiteracy, and poverty. Recently, poverty has become the number one persistent enemy. The government's development strategy has prioritized the people and providing for basic needs through improving the infrastructure.

This study advances the following four major reasons why poverty alleviation has not been achieved:
1. Pricing
2. Role of Government
3. Nature of Domestic Markets
4. The Pattern of Public Investment in Technology

The international prices of Kenyan agricultural trade commodities are directly affected by the price of imports. The prices of foreign imports are based on border price criterion. This criterion is the world price of free—on—board exports, in addition to the cost of insurance, freight for imports, and the conversion from foreign prices into domestic prices at the prevailing exchange rate. This border price typically needs to be adjusted to bring it into comparison with domestic prices like retail prices, wholesale prices, or farm—gate prices. When adjusted to the farm—gate prices, we obtain both export and import prices. Poverty was not reduced because the prices of imports have been rising compared to the prices of exports.

The government uses taxes and transaction costs to influence prices in both the informal and formal sectors and creates two markets with different prices. The price of a food crop in the formal market depends on the official consumer price of the food crop minus the marketing cost of the official agency.

The differing nature of domestic markets for food and export crops has not been adequately examined. Rural farmers sell low to the government in the informal sector. The government in turn sells high to consumers in the formal sector. Poverty has not been alleviated because the farmer is not able to obtain any of the benefits of the high prices that the formal market is willing to pay.

The size of overall agricultural output is directly affected by the pattern of public investment in technological change. Technology in the agricultural sector is fundamental to the achievement of overall increase in output, and therefore to the alleviation of poverty. What this means is, if the expenditures were directed to-

7

wards agricultural technology, then rural transport and communications, education and training of the rural entrepreneurial class, and production of rural commodities would increase.

The above determinants of poverty will be analyzed empirically using time series data for Kenya.

Contemporary Relevance

In developing countries, studies of income distribution are crucial because of inequality and the ramifications it causes such as political unrest. Inequality can cause volatile political conflicts. It is unethical and creates injustice. Income inequality constrains the freedom and opportunity of low income people. With income inequality, the political ideas acceptable to the poor have a smaller chance for success. Studies on poverty can help governments to design programs and measures to combat poverty and inequality. In order to attain this, some knowledge about the trends, patterns, and structure of income distribution as well as the determinants of inequality are necessary. Where there *is* more income equality in society, one will see more freedom to express one's views, freedom to travel within and outside the country and to participate in a socially desirable process of change, and freedom to organize for the cause of the poor as well as for the common poor.

Economically, understanding inequality will influence the structure of demand for final commodities. Income distribution determines the savings ratio of an economy and hence influences growth.

There are other reasons for interest in inequality studies. The lack of any consistent diffusion of ideas and concerns is costly. A low rate of innovation condemns the majority of the people to spend more of their time trying to survive and the bulk of their income on food.

There is an interest in income distribution studies in order to design redistribution programs and measures that will bring about social capital formation of a type that can raise productivity and consequently the income of the poor.

This book is comparable with other books published in agricultural economics and economic development specializing in Africa. Other fields are: Poverty Economics, Economics of HIV/AIDS, African Political Economy, and Growth and Income Distribution. It can be used as a text in any of the above minor fields.

Book Summary

Chapter I of this book, "Poverty," analyses the historical and current nature, extent, causes, determination, definition and measurement of poverty in Kenya. The methodology of measuring inequality incorporates a variety of approaches, including the axiomatic, the stochastic, and statistical inference.

Chapter II, "Theories of Economics," discusses the relevance of income distribution theory to development. It is stated that for the study of income distribution in Africa some aspects from each of the classical, neoclassical and Keynesian distribution theories are relevant. Accordingly, it is argued that within the arena of the developing countries, the mode of state intervention will be the determining factor for both income distribution and economic growth.

Chapter III, "Agriculture," is a theoretical analysis of the peasant agricultural sector and how an economically rational peasant farmer might make production decisions. This analysis is important because 60% of GNP in most Sub—Saharan countries is derived form the agricultural sector.

Through the results of the field survey and the discussion of the structure of the rural economy, we can find the relative importance of various crops, market orientations, constraints on production, and how production is diversified.

Many scholars and policy makers have argued that Agriculture is the key to poverty alleviation issues, yet no substantive investigation of this theory has been done to provide real data. Using an econometric model in chapter III, we will investigate the following variables in relation to Agricultural development and the validation of this hypothesis of poverty alleviation. This analysis identifies and investigates seven variables in the formation of poverty:

1. Technology in public investments
2. Land available for export crops
3. Labor devoted to the agricultural sector
4. Expenditure on essential imports
5. The level of technology in export crops

The minimization of poverty is equivalent to the maximization of rural nominal income. Thus our problem consists of determining the nominal income of households which will be maximized using an alternative mathematical model. The above variables are maximized because it would lead to increase in exports. Increase in export leads to increase in rural household income, which in turn reduces poverty.

Chapter IV, "The Socio—Economic Impact of HIV/ AIDS in Africa," describes the magnitude of the disease and how it has impacted macro sectors such as agriculture, education, business and the household.

The last part of this chapter is a modeling of macroeconomic impact of HIV/AIDS in Africa. This model provides a description of the economy. It identifies a set of technical, behavioral, and accounting variables that describe how production is organized, how individuals, businesses, and governments behave, and how the major economic variables add up.

When combined with projections of variables determined outside the model – such as weather patterns, average rainfall, tourist arrivals, petroleum prices, foreign aid flows, demographic trends, and so on – this macroeconomic model yields projections of GDP, employment, and other variables that are closely watched by policy makers and others interested in the economy's performance. The reduction in the key macroeconomic variables leads to increases in poverty as a result of HIV/AIDS. Inputs to this model are based on the output from projections the model formulates on the basis of socio—cultural and behavioral factors. The projections can be used to increase awareness of the economic impact of the problem and aid in government policy formulation. Africans cannot develop without reducing the spread of AIDS. As long as AIDS increases, poverty increases.

Chapter V is the summary and conclusion of the issues raised in Chapter I — IV. Based on the issues discussed in the preceding chapters, policy recommendations are provided on how to alleviate poverty.

I. Poverty

Summary of Growth and Distribution

1.   DEFINITION OF POVERTY

The objective of this study is to investigate the causes of poverty. In Kenya, past and present studies have concluded that the majority of the total population live below the defined poverty line. These studies on poverty analyzed the extent and its magnitude and finally all gave the definition of what constitutes poverty in the Kenyan context. Various data on poverty and income distribution in Kenya were reviewed by Ghai, Godfrey and Lisk (1979), Livingstone (1981), Collier and Lal (1981), Greer and Thorbecke (1983), Hunt (1984) and Central Bureau of Statistics small farm Integrated Rural Survey (IRS) 1994. All these studies concluded that nearly 60% of the rural population in Kenya were living below the defined poverty line[1]. In defining poverty these studies used minimum calorie consumption and monetary expenditure necessary for an adult individual to meet basic needs[2].

In 1994, the Central Bureau of Statistics presented their findings of their study on poverty. They confirmed the earlier studies that poverty in Kenya affects the majority of the population. The study defined poverty in terms of minimum calorie consumption and expenditure requirement. Poverty line was derived in two ways; absolute and relative. An absolute poverty line is fixed over time and space, i.e., over the entire area and period covered in the study. A relative poverty line is the cost of food expenditure. The measurement of poverty used is the "head count ratio" which is the incidence of poverty and the ratio of the number of poor individuals to the total population[3]. In order to justify and support the claims made that poverty exist in Kenya, the following two tables of statistics are used.

TABLE 1 shows a basket of goods a Kenyan adult should consume in 1992 to meet daily requirements. Column 2 shows monthly expenditure per capita for each item, which is then divided by unit price in column 6 to obtain kilograms consumed. The percentage of the total calorific intake (column 4), attributed to each item, is then applied to the required minimum calorific intake of 2250 k/cal. Using the consumption pattern indicated by the household's total minimum food expenditure necessary to achieve the minimum calorific intake requirement is Shs. 87.47 per capita. This amount was used to make the conclusion that the majority of the Kenyan population lives below the poverty line in 1992.

TABLE 1.1　　　　**National Monthly Rural Food Poverty Line per Adult Equivalent,**

1991/1992

Food Item	Monthly Consumption Calories Expense (Shs)	Calorie Produced	Calories Produced as % of Total Intake	Quantities Needed to Meet Requirements (kg/mnth)	Prices Kshs. /kg	Food Expend. Per month at Poverty Line (shs)
Bread	2	1288	2	46	4.3	2
Maize	24	55445	5	11.56	1.83	21
Cereals	4	5717	7	1.50	2.69	4
Meat	11	1618	2	0.70	13.72	10
Oils and Fats	2	3078	4	0.30	16.27	5
Fruits	13	1082	1	1.04	3.11	3
Vegetables	1	1248	2	2.70	2.24	6
Beans	6	5784	7	1.61	4.99	5
Roots	7	3345	4	2.07	2.49	8
Sugar	9	7.19	7	1.29	5.45	7
Tea/Coffee	8	27	0.03	0.10	19.06	2
Eggs	4	187	0.24	0.12	7.88	1
Milk	2	3256	4	3.52	3.30	12
Total	101	78044	100			87

Source: Economic Survey p.55, Kenya Government Printer, 1997

The studies have identified the possible causes of poverty to be investigated as:
　　　　　A)　　　　The role of prices in both international and domestic terms of trade

B)   Stagnant technical change in agriculture
C)   Domestic changes in prices, between food crops and export crops.
D)   The role of government intervention in creating multiple markets and prices.

At the aggregate level, Kenyan rural households derived 57.9 percent of their incomes from farm sources, 10.4 percent from non—farm, 23.1 percent from salaries/wages, and 9.7 percent from other sources. In comparison, the absolute poor, defined as those below the absolute poverty line, derived 63.0 percent of their incomes from farm sources, this is depicted in TABLE 2.

TABLE 1.2 Sources of Income by Rural Poverty Group, 1981/82: Absolute Poverty Line (Shs 105.94)

	All	Non—Poor	Poor	All %	Non—Poor %	Poor %
Farm	444.18	538.69	308.04	57.93	56.15	62.98
Non—Farm	79.33	100.73	48.50	10.35	10.50	9.92
Sal-ary/Wages	176.73	240.31	85.13	23.05	25.05	17.41
Other Income	66.47	79.71	47.40	8.67	8.31	9.69
Total	766.71	959.44	489.08	100.00	100.00	100.00

Source: Statistical Abstract: Ministry of Planning and National Development p.186

2.   METHODOLOGY

Although Central Bureau of Statistics has made considerable progress in recent years, Kenya like most developing countries, still has data limitations particularly relating to the production and consumption of stable food crops. The level of aggregation of existing data is frequently too high to permit much flexibility in their use. Sometimes the available data have been obtained through techniques that suggest results that are of little value for meaningful analysis. For example, with some sample survey figures as base, acreage data for other years are obtained as projections, on the assumption that land cultivation expands at the same rate as population. With this type of data, however, it is impossible to study the acreage responses that a given farm population might make when demand conditions for their products change.

Apart from this, population data for Kenya are a continuing source of controversy, and the assumed rate of growth is at best an "educated guess" subject to an intolerably wide margin of error. The situation is made even more intractable by the fact that most of the food crops are planted in sole stands as well as in mixed stands (inter—cropped) along with other food crops. Thus changes in the output of any given food crop may not always be correlated with variations in total acreage under crops.

As a result of this unsatisfactory data situation the author conducted a field survey in three provinces in Kenya (Nyanza, Rift Valley, Eastern) in July 1996. This consisted of questionnaire interviews of two—hundred farmers in sixteen villages in six districts in respective provinces. (A fairly detailed description of the survey method will be found in APPENDIX A, the interview schedule is in APPENDIX B.)

The peasant agricultural population was therefore divided into four strata according to the relative importance of crops in each area. This stratification was justified by the following reasoning: If export expansion has had an impact on food production, such impact ought to be greater in the areas where exports have been expanded the most. The first stratum consisted of sixteen villages near the rift valley province which is ecologically suited for tea and coffee. The second stratum consisted of a group of villages in the northeastern province. This stratum occupies an intermediate position where tree crops do grow but have been neglected due to the constraints given in the APPENDIX B

TABLE 1.3
Percentage Distribution of Export Crops and Food Crops by District

Crop	Kericho No.	%	Nandi No.	%	Baringo No.	%	Keiyo No.	%
Export	180	90	135	83	129	40	188	50
Import	200	100	200	100	181	100	200	100

Source: Compiled by Author

Inequality Measurement

1.   THE AXIOMATIC APPROACH.

The Pigou—Dalton Transfer Principle (Dalton, 1920). Consider the vector y' which is a transformation of the vector y obtained by a transfer δ from y_j to y_i, where $y_i > y_j$, and $y_i + \delta > y_j - \delta$, then the transfer principle is satisfied if $I(y') \geq I(y)$.

Income Scale Independence. Hence for any scalar $\lambda > 0$, $I(y) = I(\lambda \, y)$. Again most standard measures pass this test except the variance since $var(\lambda \, y) = \lambda^2 var(y)$.

Principle of Population (Dalton, 1920). For any scalar $\lambda > 0$, $I(y) = I(y[\lambda])$, where $y[\lambda]$ is a concatenation of the vector y, λ times.

Anonymity. Hence for any permutation y' of y, $I(y) = I(y')$.

Decomposability. Some measures, such as the Generalized Entropy class of measures, are easily decomposed and into intuitively appealingly components of within—group inequality and between—group inequality: $I_{total} = I_{within} + I_{between}$.

Members of the Generalized Entropy class of measures have the general formula as follows:

$$GE(\alpha) = \frac{1}{\alpha^2 - \alpha} \left[\frac{1}{n} \sum_{i-1}^{n} \left(\frac{y_i}{\overline{y}} \right)^n - 1 \right] \quad (1.1)$$

where n is the number of individuals in the sample. The commonest values of α used are 0, 1 and 2: hence a value of $\alpha = 0$ gives more weight to distances between incomes in the lower tail, $\alpha = 1$ applies equal weights across the distribution, while a value of $\alpha = 2$ gives proportionately more weight to gaps in the upper tail. Two of Theil's measures of inequality (Theil, 1967), the mean log deviation and the Theil index respectively, as follows:

$$GE(0) = \frac{1}{n} \sum_{i-1}^{n} \log \frac{\overline{y}}{y_i}$$

$$GE(1) = \frac{1}{n} \sum_{i-1}^{n} \frac{y_i}{\overline{y}} \log \frac{y_i}{\overline{y}} \quad (1.2)$$

With $\alpha = 2$ the GE measure becomes ½ the squared coefficient of variation, CV:

$$CV = \frac{1}{\overline{y}} \left[\frac{1}{n} \sum_{i-1}^{n} (y_i - \overline{y})^2 \right]^{\frac{1}{2}}$$

The Atkinson class of measures has the general formula:

$$A_x = 1 - \left[\frac{1}{n} \sum_{i-1}^{n} \left[\frac{y_1}{\bar{y}} \right]^{1-\delta} \right]^{\frac{1}{(1-\delta)}} \qquad (1.3)$$

The Gini coefficient satisfies axioms 1— 4 above, but will fail the decomposability axiom if the sub—vectors of income overlap. There are ways of decomposing the Gini but the component terms of total inequality are not always intuitive or mathematically appealing (see for example Fei et al, 1978, and an attempt at a decomposition with a more intuitive residual term by Yitzhaki and Lerman, 1991). However the Gini's popularity merits it mention here. It is defined as follows (Gini, 1912):

$$Gini = \frac{1}{2n^2 \bar{y}} \sum_{i=l}^{n} \sum_{j=l}^{n} \left| y_i - y_j \right| \qquad (1.4)$$

The Gini coefficient takes on values between zero and one with zero interpreted as no inequality.

Using the Gini coefficient, Table ... shows the inequality measurements in the continent of Africa.

TABLE 1.4   Poverty Index for the Continent of Africa

Country	Survey Yr.	Gini Index*	Lowest 10%	Lowest 20%	Second 20%	High-est 20%	High-est 10%
Algeria	1995	35.3	2.8	7.0	11.6	42.6	26.8
Burkina Faso	1998	55.1	2.0	4.6	7.2	60.4	46.8
Burundi	1998	42.5	1.8	5.1	10.3	48.0	32.9
Country	Survey Yr.	Gini Index*	Lowest 10%	Lowest 20%	Second 20%	High-est 20%	High-est 10%
Camer-oon	1996	47.7	1.9	4.6	8.3	53.1	36.6
Central African Rep.	1993	61.3	0.7	2.0	4.9	65.0	47.7
Egypt	1995	28.9	4.4	9.8	13.2	39.0	25.0
Ethiopia	1995	40.0	3.0	7.1	10.9	47.7	33.7
Gambia	1998	50.2	1.6	4.0	7.6	55.3	38.2
Ghana	1999	40.7	2.2	5.6	10.0	46.7	30.1
Guinea	1994	40.3	2.6	6.4	10.4	47.2	32.0
Guinea—Bissau	1991	56.2	0.5	2.1	6.5	58.9	42.4
Kenya	1997	44.9	2.4	5.6	9.3	51.2	36.1
Lesotho	1986,7	56.0	0.9	2.8	6.5	60.1	43.4

16

Mada-gascar	1999	38.1	2.6	6.4	10.7	44.9	28.6
Mali	1994	50.5	1.8	4.6	8.0	56.2	40.4
Maurita-nia	1995	37.3	2.5	6.4	11.2	44.1	28.4
Morocco	1998	39.5	2.6	6.5	10.6	46.6	30.9
Mozam-bique	1996	39.6	2.5	6.5	10.8	46.5	31.7
Niger	1995	50.5	0.8	2.6	7.1	53.3	35.4
Nigeria	1996	50.6	1.6	4.4	8.2	55.7	40.8
Rwanda	1983—5	28.9	4.2	9.7	13.2	39.1	24.2
Senegal	1995	41.3	2.6	6.4	10.3	48.2	33.5
Sierra Leone	1989	62.9	0.5	1.1	2.0	63.4	43.6
South Africa	1993,4	59.3	1.1	2.9	5.5	64.8	45.9
Swazi-land	1994	60.9	1.0	2.7	5.8	64.4	50.2
Tanzania	1993	38.2	2.8	6.8	11.0	45.5	30.1
Tunisia	1995	41.7	2.3	5.7	9.9	47.9	31.8
Uganda	1996	37.4	3.0	7.1	11.1	44.9	29.8
Zambia	1998	52.6	1.1	3.3	7.6	56.6	41.0
Zim-babwe	1995	50.1	2.0	4.7	8.0	55.7	40.4

Source World Bank
* *Gini Index* measures the extent to which the distribution of income (or, in some cases, consumption expenditure) among individuals or households within an economy deviates from a perfectly equal distribution. A Lorenz curve plots the cumulative percentages of total income received against the poorest individual or houSehold. The Gini Index measures the area between the Lorenz curve and a hypothetical line of absolute equality, expressed as a percentage of the maximum area under the line. Thus a Gini index of zero represents perfect equality, while an index of one—hundred implies perfect inequality.

- Data of distribution compiled by the World Bank's Development Research Group
- Data for highest income economies compiled by the Luxaembourg Income Study database.
- Many African nations aren't included due to difficulties in data collection.

2.   AN ALTERNATIVE APPROACH: STOCHASTIC DOMINANCE

First order stochastic dominance. Consider two income distributions y_1 and y_2 with cumulative distribution functions (CDFs) $F(y_1)$ and $F(y_2)$. If $F(y_1)$ lies nowhere above and at least somewhere below $F(y_2)$ then distribution y_1 displays first order stochastic dominance over distribution y_2: $F(y_1) \leq F(y_2)$ for all y. Hence in distribution y_1 there are no more individuals with income less than a given income level than in distribution y_2, for all levels of income. We can express this in an alternative way using the inverse function $y = F^{-1}(p)$ where p is the share of the population with income less than a given income level: first order dominance is attained if $F_1^{-1}(p) \geq F_2^{-1}(p)$ for all p. The inverse function $F^{-1}(p)$ is known as a Pen's Parade (Pen, 1974 which simply plots incomes against cumulative population, usually using ranked income quantiles. The dominant distribution is that whose Parade lies nowhere below and at least somewhere above the other. First order stochastic dominance of distribution y_1 over y_2 implies that any social wel-

17

fare function that is increasing in income, will record higher levels of welfare in distribution $\mathbf{y}_1$ than in distribution $\mathbf{y}_2$ (Saposnik, 1981, 1983).

Second order stochastic dominance. Consider now the deficit functions (the integral of the CDF) of distributions $\mathbf{y}_1$ and $\mathbf{y}_2$:

$$G(y_{i,k}) = \int_0^{y_1} F(y_1)dy \qquad (1.5)$$

i = 1, 2. If the deficit function of distribution $\mathbf{y}_1$ lies nowhere above and somewhere below that of distribution $\mathbf{y}_2$, then distribution $\mathbf{y}_1$ displays second order stochastic dominance over distribution $\mathbf{y}_2$: $G(\mathbf{y}_{1,k}) \leq G(\mathbf{y}_{2,k})$ for all y_k. The dual of the deficit curve is the Generalized Lorenz curve (Shorrocks, 1983) defined as:

$$GL(p) = \int_0^{y_i} ydF(y) \qquad (1.6)$$

which plots cumulative income shares scaled by the mean of the distribution against cumulative population, where the height of the curve at p is given by the mean of the distribution below p. As Atkinson and Bourguignon (1989) and Howes (1993) have shown, second order dominance established by comparisons of the deficit curves for complete, uncensored distributions implies and is implied by Generalized Larenz dominance: $GL_1(\mathbf{p}) \geq GL_2(\mathbf{p})$ for all $\mathbf{p}$. Second order dominance of distribution $\mathbf{y}_1$ over distribution $\mathbf{y}_2$ implies that any social welfare function that is increasing and concave in income will record higher levels of welfare in $\mathbf{y}_1$ than $\mathbf{y}_2$ (Shorrocks, 1983). It should now be apparent that second order stochastic dominance is therefore implied by first order stochastic dominance, although the reverse is not true.

Mean—normalized second order stochastic dominance. In order to rank distributions in terms of inequality alone, rather than welfare, a third concept (also known as Lorenz dominance) is applied. If the Lorenz curve, the plot of cumulative income shares against cumulative population shares, of distribution $\mathbf{y}_1$ lies nowhere below and at least somewhere above the Lorenz curve of distribution $\mathbf{y}_2$ then $\mathbf{y}_1$ Lorenz dominates $\mathbf{y}_2$. Any inequality measure which satisfies anonymity and the Pigou—Dalton transfer principle will rank the two distributions in the same way as the Lorenz curves (Atkinson, 1970).

3.   STATISTICAL INFERENCE AND SAMPLING VARIANCE

For example the Atkinson class can be written as:

$$A_\delta = 1 - \frac{\left[\mu_\gamma'\right]^{1/\gamma}}{\mu_1'} \qquad (1.7)$$

where μ_r' is the rth moment about zero, r=1—ε and μ_1'= the mean of the distribution,

and the GE class as:

$$GE(\alpha) = \frac{1}{\alpha^2 - \alpha}\left[\mu_{1\alpha}\left[\mu_{11}\right]^{-\alpha}\left[\mu_{10}\right]^{\alpha-1} - 1\right], \alpha \neq 0,1 \qquad (1.8)$$

where $\mu \, v \, \alpha$ are the moments about zero defined as:

$$\mu_{v\alpha} = \int\int z^v y^u \, dF(z,y) \qquad 1.9$$

where z is household size (or some other weighting variable), v = 1, 2 and $-\infty < \alpha < \infty$. The sample moments mv α can be expressed as mv $\alpha = \frac{1}{n}\sum z_i^v y_{i\alpha}$. If both mean household size and mean income are known, then Var(GE(α)) is relatively easy to derive:

$$\hat{V} = \frac{1}{[n-1][\alpha^2 - \alpha]^2}\left[m_{11}\right]^{-2\alpha}\left[m_{10}\right]^{2\alpha-2}\left[m_{2,2\alpha} - m_{1\alpha}^2\right] \quad (1.10)$$

For the full details of the method and for the cases where α = 0 and 1, and where the population mean income and household size are not known see Cowell (1989, 1995).

It is also possible to test the statistical significance of any stochastic dominance results. Howes (1993) describes one test based on a simple test of sample mean differences:

$$z_i = \frac{\hat{\xi} - \hat{\xi}_i^*}{\left(\dfrac{\hat{C}_{ii}}{N} + \dfrac{\hat{C}_{ii}^*}{N^*}\right)^{1/2}} \qquad (1.11)$$

where $\xi = (\xi_1, \ldots \xi_w)$ is a vector of heights of curves (Pen's Parades, Lorenz or Generalized Lorenz curves), C_{ii} is the relevant element in the diagonal of the vari-

19

ance—covariance matrix associated with ξ and N is the sample size. Z_i is asymptotically normally distributed. See Howes (1993) for fuller details and an empirical application to China, and Ferreira and Litchfield (1996) for an application to Brazil.

SUMMARY: GROWTH AND DISTRIBUTION

In sum, income and wealth distributions can no longer be seen as mere outcomes of the general equilibrium of an economy. The central processes that determine resource allocation – through capital markets, through the political system, and through social circumstances – are influenced by the distribution of wealth in important ways. More unequal societies tend to develop larger groups of people who are excluded from opportunities others enjoy – be they a better education, access to loans, or to insurance – and who therefore do not develop their full productive potentials. Both theory and empirical evidence suggest that these incomplete realizations of economic potential are not of concern only to those who care about equity per se. They also affect aggregate economic potential, and therefore aggregate output and its rate of growth.

The inverted—U relationship between growth and inequality suggested by Kuznets has not survived recent empirical scrutiny terribly well. Instead, it is gradually being replaced by a perception that the main flow of causation may be in the other direction, with inequality hampering the rate and quality of economic growth. The debate is not over, either conceptually or empirically. But its very liveliness attests to the importance of the question. To paraphrase Tony Atkinson, inequality is unlikely to go back out into the cold periphery of economic analysis any time in the foreseeable future.

II. ECONOMIC THEORIES

Classical Theories of Income Distribution

1.   ADAM SMITH

Adam Smith never presented a detailed, integrated model of economic growth. His *Nature and Causes of the Wealth of Nations* was intended to explain how a nations' economy could increase the wealth of its citizens, and economic growth is discussed in many ways throughout the book. Smith suggests two distinct sources of economic growth, one directly linked to the increase in specialization, the other related to the level of specialization.

Every time specialization increases, there are new gains from exchange as individuals, firms, and entire countries exploit the gains from comparative advantage and increasing returns to scale. These gains in specialization may be due to sudden changes in institution, transportation improvements, or sudden breakthroughs in human knowledge. But, perhaps more importantly, as the level of specialization increases, individuals and firms are more likely to "discover easier and readier methods of attaining any object, when the whole attention of their minds is directed towards the single object, than when it is dissipated among a great variety of things".[1] That is, total learning by doing and R & D efforts increase with the level of specialization and, therefore, cause the rate of change in technology to increase. Many of these gains in technology, in turn, permit further specialization. Smith sees economic growth as continuing forever, likely to even increase as specialization becomes ever greater.

We depict the Smithian growth model graphically in Figure 1. Suppose the level of per capita income at time 0 is equal to A, the result of previous increases in specialization and innovation. As time passes, innovation, research, discovery, and learning by doing are continually taking place. Between time 0 and time 1, per capita income grows to B as the economy traces out the growth path Ab. At time 1, suppose that the introduction of money permits a sudden increase in specialization, which raises per capita income to C. Then, innovation, research, discovery, and learning by doing continue at a higher rate because specialization is greater and, thus, allows for an even greater "direction of the minds towards single objects". Note that the segment cd of the economy's growth path rises at a more rapid rate than it did before the increase in specialization.

Suppose that there is a second institutional change, at time two, say, the elimination of war between neighboring countries, that permits international trade where none had been possible before. There will be another sudden jump in specialization, which will cause per capita income to rise from D to E. The economy's growth path then continues further at an even more rapid pace after time two.

Smith's optimistic model of economic growth thus consists of a series of discrete jumps and a gradually increasing underlying rate of technological progress.

21

The sudden discrete rises in per capita output are the result of increases in specialization caused by improved transportation or institutional changes. The increased slope of the smooth sections of the curve represents continuous innovation, research, and learning by doing, which are a function of the degree of specialization. Increases in specialization drive technology growth, and technology growth in turn drives further specialization.

FIGURE 2.1 Smith Growth Mode

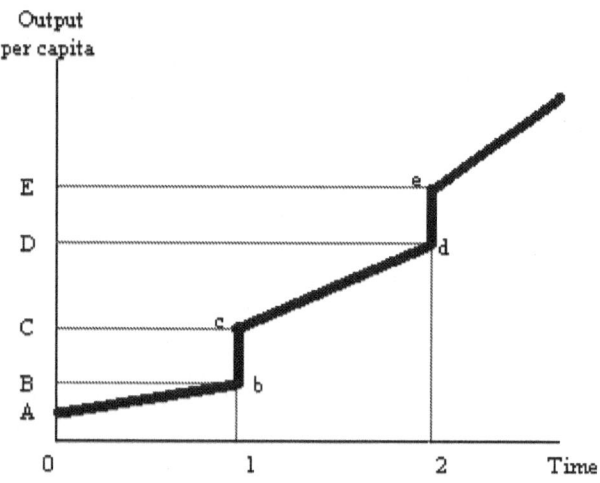

Source: Van Den Berg, Economic Growth and Development. P.94

Institutional improvements, such as money, legal protection of property rights, and more personal freedom to make economic choices, provide further boosts to the growth of per capita income.

In summarizing Adam Smith's work, it is difficult to overestimate his influence on the development of economic thought in general and growth theory in particular. As we examine some of the principal growth theories that were subsequently developed, we should keep in mind several of the key points Adam Smith made in the Wealth of Nations:

- Specialization and exchange must increase if the economy is to grow.
- Markets where transactions are voluntary result in individuals and firms making decisions that are compatible with the "general welfare".
- There is a close association between specialization and the generation of new technology and knowledge because specialization promotes what we would now refer to as learning by doing and intentional investment in R & D.

- The bottom line in judging the performance of an economy is human welfare throughout the entire population. This points to the need for analysis that can capture all the changes that occur throughout the economy.

Adam Smith may have put too much economics into one work; had he written a concise volume on just economic growth, he would probably be heralded today as the father of growth economics as well as the father of economics. Adam Smith's incredible understanding of so many areas of economics left the door open for others to focus their attention on specific issues such as economic growth. Unfortunately, some of the other early economists left us with a much less optimistic picture of the growth process than the one Adam Smith gave us.

Application for African Growth

Based on the Smithian analysis, we can conclude that some of its facets are applicable to Africa's growth path. Smith said that countries should specialize in goods that have absolute advantage. If Africa adopts a Smithian model of specialization of goods, then they will be competitive in the global arena.

However, for Smith's theory of absolute advantage to work, Africa must extend the Smithian model using the Ricardian Theory of comparative advantage, which says that countries should specialize according to their relative productivities.

2.   MARXIAN THEORY

Marx adopted the classical utility concept into his own analysis. Marx made distinction between use—value and exchange value as the center of his economics.

According to Marx an object cannot be produced unless it is useful or satisfies a particular need and therefore has a use—value. The utility of a thing makes it a use value. Marx viewed use value as an intrinsic virtue of objects as material quality. But from neo—classical notion use—value is a relation of subject to object and becomes a judgment passed on the object by the subject. Use—value in itself objective from the Marxian perspective. Being limited by the physical properties of the commodity, it has no existence apart form that commodity (Marx, Volume 1 pp. 36)

Use value is based on the intrinsic characteristics of the commodity as he put it "As use—values, commodities are above all, of different qualities, but as exchange—values they are merely different quantities (volume I, pp. 37—38)

According to Marx, because use—values are qualities, each is different from the other, therefore they cannot be compared. Use—values cannot then exchanged for use—values because exchange implicitly means comparison and thus the possibility of finding an equivalence between quantities. It is also, true that only a commodity with use—value con have exchange—value since only commodities that have utility will be exchanged.

Marx explained that the measure of value exists before exchange. "It becomes plain, that it is not the exchange of commodities with regulates the magnitude of their value which controls their exchange proportions." In order to compare various commodities with different use—values the exchange values of commodities must be measured in terms of labor values or labor time embedded in them.

Just as Adam Smith created much of the foundation for capitalist thought, Karl Marx is responsible for the foundation of planned socialism. Marx's theory of history sought to explain the evolution of socialism and, for that reason, we will briefly examine the principles he set forth. This is true even though Marx wrote mostly about Capitalism rather than socialism. Indeed, his most important work, Das Kapital, is an analysis of capitalism and a forecast by Marx of its ultimate demise.

The philosophical foundation of Marxism is dialectical materialism, a philosophy that views material things as the subject of all change and technology, and the natural environment as the main forces that cause human society to change continually. Let's examine this philosophy one step at a time.

FIGURE 2.2   An Example of Marxian Analysis

Dialectical Materialism

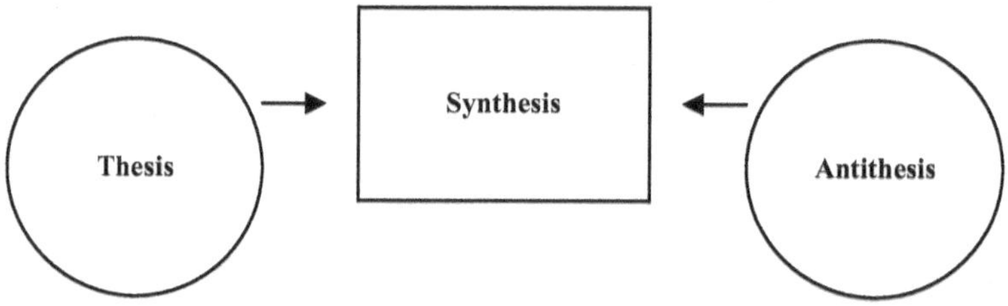

Dialectics emphasizes that all phenomena, natural and human, involve processes of development. The seed grows into the plant. The infant grows into the child, the child into the youth, the youth into the adult. (Darwin's theory of evolution is another example of the dialectical process of reasoning.)

Marx analyzed this process of development of human society, and used it, as he came to understand it, as the scientific basis for socialism. The first law of this argument is that the foundation of society is materialistic. Technology and the natural environment (climate, resources, geography) are the dominant forces in society's development. The rest (culture, institutions, social classes, and the relations between them) are linked to the economic (materialist) base, and are shaped by that base.

Dialectical materialism is the basic idea behind Marx's concept of Historical materialism, which holds that human society throughout history has undergone a continual process of change, or development from one form to another: this change results from conflict between classes in a society. In ancient times, there was slavery; in medieval times, serfdom; then came handicraft and cottage industry, which gave way to factory—oriented capitalism. The guiding factors in this process are changing technology and the natural environment.

The above example illustrates this process of social change or class conflict for the transition from feudalism to the beginnings of capitalism. The *thesis* (the class system that is dominant at a given time) is feudalism, in which the ruling class is the landed aristocracy. The *antithesis* (the class that is the main force in changing the thesis) is the emerging commercial changes) is mercantile capitalism, in which the commercial class replaces the landed aristocracy as the dominant class.

Marx, as we indicated before, believed that the most dramatic feature of this process of change was the conflict of classes at each stage of development. In ancient Rome, the slaves were in conflict with their masters. In medieval Europe, the serfs and the emerging merchant class were in conflict with the landed aristocracy. With the development of factories, a new class, the *proletariat* (the workers in the factories), came into conflict with the capitalists, the owners of the factories. The basis of these conflicts is the effort of one class to dominate and exploit other classes. A basic tenet of Marxism is that as long as there are private property rights classes will continue to exist, and conflict will result. Marx argued for a labor theory of value, which is that all value is created by labor, but that wages under capitalism tend toward a subsistence level. The difference between the value of products created by labor and the wage payments to labor constituted what Marx called surplus value.

According to Marx, competition between firms and the increasing scarcity of profitable investment opportunities would cause profits in a capitalist economy to fall. Capitalists could counter this fall in two ways: (1) They could get employees to work longer hours, and in this way increase surplus value and the degree of exploitation of labor. But the opportunity to do this was limited. (2) They could invest more and improve technology further, thus increasing output per worker and surplus value. However, improving technology meant that more and more machines replaced more and more workers, and this increased unemployment.

The rising number of unemployed caused by increased use of capital and improved technology was called the reserve army of the unemployed. This reserve army, Marx said, competed with the employed workers, and this competition had the effect of keeping wages down.

Marx also maintained that as capitalists increase investment to ward off falling profits, the productive capacity of the economy expands and output increases. But because wages are kept low, workers do not have the ability to buy this expanded output. So, although the economy expands for a while, eventually industry's ability to produce output far outstrips consumers' ability to buy that growing output. (If you tool up your factory with all the latest equipment, so that you can make ten—thousand washing machines a month, but the public has enough purchasing power to buy only five—thousand of them, you will eventually go broke.) Excess capacity is generated, which causes economic crisis and then collapse. Along comes a depression, and firms are forced out of business. Eventually, enough firms are forced out of business so that capacity contracts to a point at which expansion can be renewed, and the process repeats itself. Marx identified the business cycle and the exploitation of labor as the two hallmarks of the capitalist system. Marx was one of the first to introduce the idea of recurring business cycles, and his theory of them constituted a significant contribution to economic theory.

Marx concluded that capitalism (the thesis) contained within it inherent contradictions (capitalism's antithesis) that would bring about its end and a movement toward the next stage of development, socialism. He predicted that economic crises would recur, and would become progressively more serious. With more investment and continuing technological change, the reserve army of the unemployed would become larger and larger. Because of their increased investment and ever—greater need to compete against others, firms would get bigger. As this occurred, those among the bourgeoisie who owned smaller firms would be forced into the proletariat and into the reserve army of the unemployed. Eventually, Marx predicted economic crisis and unemployment would become so large that revolution would take place and capitalism would be overthrown. The proletariat would come to realize that capitalism was against their self—interest; the wastes of resources due to recurring crises would become apparent. The proletariat would therefore seize political power and establish a socialist society, which would ultimately evolve into a classless communist society.

Application for African Growth:
After analyzing Marxian economics, one may conclude that it is problematic. It is very difficult to apply to the specific African context. Marx advocated the principle of reward for people's contribution to society. It is very difficult to measure such a contribution across professions and across cultures.

Marx did, however, point out very relevant issues. His analysis of exploitation of the working class by the capitalist points to the need to explore possibilities for correcting the anomaly of inequality in society. He points to the driving force of capitalist society as being profits, leading to social stratification. The rich get richer and the poor get poorer. Using a Marxist analysis to look at profit in Africa will be helpful to anyone seeking to address the issues of inequality.

Neoclassical Theories of Income Distribution

1.   SOLOW – MODEL

Output, in the Solow model, is a function of capital and labor:

$$Y = F(K, L),$$

$$(2.1)$$

and the production function, F, is assumed to satisfy three properties.

26

First, it exhibits constant returns to scale. That is, for all $\lambda \geq 0, F(\lambda K, \lambda L) = \lambda F(K,L)$. It follows, by taking $\lambda = 1/L$, that

$$Y = F(k,L) = LF(k,1),$$

or

$$y = f(k),$$

$$(2.2)$$

where $y \equiv Y/L$, $k \equiv K/L$ and $f(k) \equiv F(k,1)$. (2.2) is referred to as the production function in "intensive form". It is worth noting that because of these assumptions, per capita output can grow only if the capital—labor ratio increases.

Second, $F_K, F_L > 0$ and $F_{KK}, F_{LL} < 0$. That is, the law of diminishing returns holds.

Third, F satisfies the Inada conditions:

$$\lim_{K \to 0} F_K(K,L) = \lim_{L \to 0} F_L(K,L) = \infty$$

and

$$\lim_{K \to \infty} F_K(K,L) = \lim_{L \to \infty} F_L(K,L) = 0$$

Although thus far in this section I have ignored the time subscript on variables, the subscripts are assumed to be there and will be invoked when it is important to bring in time explicitly.

We assume that the marginal propensity to save in this economy is fixed at s. Let the capital depreciation rate be δ. Hence

$$\dot{K} = sLf(k) - \delta K,$$

or

$$\frac{\dot{K}}{L} = sf(k) - \delta k.$$

Note that

$$\dot{k} = sf(k) - (\delta = n)k,$$

$$(2.3)$$

assuming, as before that $\dot{L}/L = n$, for all t. This differential equation involving the capital—labor ratio alone was called the "fundamental equation" by Solow (1956) because it captures the central idea of the neoclassical theory of growth.

In analyzing the implications of the fundamental equation it is convenient to write it as a growth rate and then analyze it diagrammatically as done by Barro and Sala—i—Martin (1995). Dividing both sides of the fundamental equation by k, we get

$$\hat{k} = \frac{sf(k)}{k} - (\delta + n).$$

(2.4)

Note that $\hat{k}$ is the growth rate of the capital—labor ratio.

Much of growth theory has been concerned with not what happens in a particular period but in the "steady state". A *steady state* is reached when the variables attain constant growth rates. To locate

Investment and
Depreciation

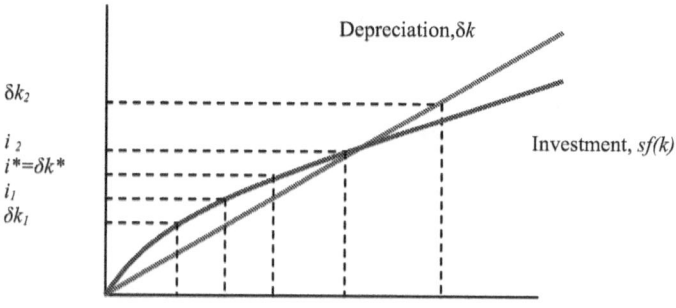

Figure 2.3

the steady state of the Solow model, draw $sf(k)/k$ as a function of k.

The shape of the graph $sf(k)/k$ is very important for the Solow model. By using the Inada condition, it can be shown that $f(k)/k$ goes to zero as k goes to infinity, and it goes to infinity as k goes to zero. To see this, note the

$$f'(k) = F_K(K,L).$$

By drawing a picture of $f(k)$ as a function of k, while keeping in mind the concavity of f and the Inada condition, in particular, that $\lim_{k \to 0} f'(k) = \infty$, the above claim about the shape of $f(k)/k$ is natural. It is formally an implication of l'Hôpital's Rule.

It now follows that the two graphs in figure 3.1 must intersect. Let k^* be the capital—labor ratio at the point of intersection. If $k = k'$, then the growth rate of k is given by AB. Because this is positive, the economy will move right at k' and the growth rate will fall. It is evident that the steady state only occurs with a growth rate of 0 and with capital—labor ratio constant at k^*.

Since $y = f(k)$, per capita income also reaches constancy, at $f(k^*)$, in the long run. And the same is true of per capita consumption, which in the steady state equals $(1 - s)f(k^*)$.

What happens if the rate of savings, s, in the economy rises? In the short run, this will raise the growth rates $\hat{k}$ and $\hat{y}$. But in the long run, these rates once again go to zero. In the new steady state per capita income is higher but the growth rate of per capita income is exactly the same as before, to wit, zero.

Economists, who have had their focus primarily on steady state growth rates, would see little benefit in raising s or any other policy for that matter because in the steady state the growth rate will always be the same. This has been one of the motivations behind the rise of endogenous growth, it is worth keeping in mind that the "short run" can last for a very long time; convergence to the steady state could easily stretch over decades. Hence we may well want to use savings and investment policy to influence growth even it in the long run the effect vanishes. The case for such intervention gets strengthened if steady state growth is endogenous and depends on the savings rate.

Application for African Growth:

After analyzing Solow's model, we can conclude that the Solow model does not directly apply to the African growth path. It works well for developed society where we find little government intervention or little government strategy for developing markets. If the markets are well developed, then Solow makes sense.

However, the Solow model's assumptions of two goods, those of the capitalist and the laborer are too simplistic for an underdeveloped market society. They are not realistic for complex society in general and would only confuse the situation in Africa.

2. MARGINAL PRODUCTIVITY THEORY

Marginal productivity theory may be described as a theory of distribution provided we remember that it has nothing to say about the supply side in factor markets. Strictly speaking, it is only a theory of the demand for a factor. This is why Alfred Marshall (1961, 517—25) objected to statements implying that the marginal productivity of a factor "determines " its rate of reward. Marginal productivity theory holds that in equilibrium each productive agent will be rewarded in accordance with its marginal productivity, as measured by the effect of the addition or withdrawal of a unit of that agent on the total product with the quantity of the other agents held fixed. John Bates Clark (1891, 313: 1899, 3), the American founder of marginal productivity theory, regarded the theory as providing a normative principle of distributive justice. Clark developed the theory within the framework of a stationary state with perfect competition, perfect foresight and perfect factor mobility. He assumed each factor to be homogeneous and that all units of the factor were equally efficient. In what follows we shall present a brief rough approximation of J. B. Clark's theory of distribution.

J. B. Clark's Distribution Theory: A Rough Sketch

Let

y = output
x = input
w = price of labor input
4   p = price of output
py = total revenue

$y = f(x), x = g(y)$
$\phi = pf(x) - wx = \Pi$ where Π = profit
$\phi'(x) = pf'(x) - w = 0$
$p = w / f'(x) = w / f'[g(y)]$, since $x = g(y)$

Since the marginal productivity theory neglects the supply side in factor markets and considers only the demand side we have the demand function for labor as shown in Figure 2.4.

Figure 2.4
Demand Function For Labor

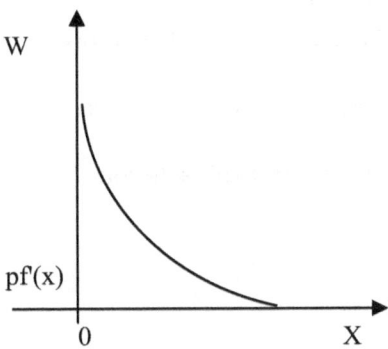

And now for the division of total output into wages and profits we have (figure 2.5):

Figure 2.5
Division of Total Output

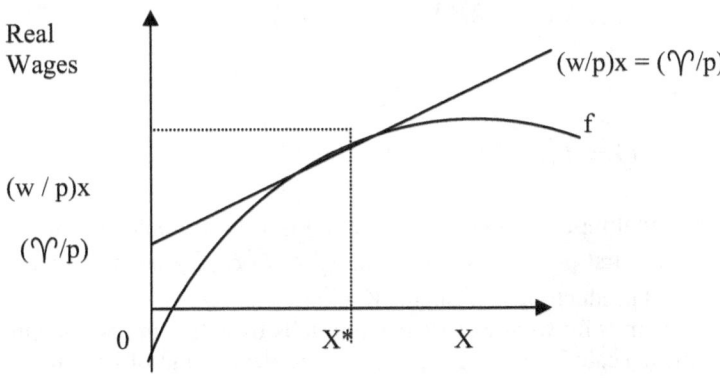

(w/p)x = real wages
Π/p = real profits

Figure 3.3 shows total output or total real national income and how it is divided up between wages and profits:

Π= py — wx
y = Π/p + wx/p

$$(x)fd = zp(z)_1 f \int_x^0 d = zp(z), fd \int_x^0$$

But $y = f(x)$

Thus $pf(x) = py$: national income

But $py = wx + \Pi$, that is, wage bill + profits

And hence share in national income can be presented as

$SHR = wx / py + \Pi$, where SHR is the total

Or

$1 = wx / py + \Pi / y$

But how are the relative shares determined? Here we have no clue from Clark's marginal productivity theory.

However, we know that under the mathematical assumption of linear homogeneity (which implies the economic assumption of constant returns to scale) Euler's theorem tells us that the total product, Q, will be exhausted if each unit employed receives its marginal physical product:

$$Q \equiv K(\partial Q / \partial K) + L(\partial Q / \partial L)$$

Where

$$Q = f(K, L)$$

K is capital input, L is labor input, and f is a linear homogeneous production function. The first partial derivatives of $Q = f(K, L)$ are the marginal products or marginal productivities of inputs K and L.

Economically what Euler's theorem tells us is that under conditions of constant returns to scale if each input factor is paid the amount of its marginal product then the total product will be exactly exhausted by the economic profit will be zero. Euler's theorem played a major role in the basic postulates of this theory are that (1) each input is paid the value of its marginal product, and (2) total output is just exhausted. Since these conditions are satisfied by production functions homogeneous of degree one, it was mistakenly assumed that all production functions must be of this type (Henderson & Quandt, 1971, 82; Chiang, 1974, 407).

The condition of product exhaustion is equivalent to the condition that maximum long—run equals zero.

Following the assumptions of the marginal productivity theory together with Euler's theorem we arrive at the startling conclusion that long—run profit equals zero regardless of the level of the product price. However, "the zero economic profit in the long—run equilibrium can be brought about by the forces of competition, including the entry and exit of firms, regardless of the specific nature of the production function actually prevailing. Moreover, when imperfect competition exists in the factor markets, the payment to the factors may not be equal to the marginal products, and consequently, Euler's theorem becomes irrelevant to the distribution picture" (Chiang, 1974, 407). Indeed, we agree with this analysis, as we also further agree with Henderson and Quandt (1971, 82) who find the analysis of the marginal productivity theory of distribution to be "misleading, if not erroneous" (Henderson & Quandt, 1971, 82). They show that the conventional analysis of profit maximization breaks down if the entrepreneur sells his output at a constant price and possesses a production function which is homogeneous of degree one. They further maintain that the assumption of a homogeneous production function is not necessary for the fulfillment of the postulates of the marginal productivity theory. These postulates can be fulfilled if the production function is not homogeneous, the first— and second—order conditions for profit maximization are fulfilled, and the entrepreneur's maximum profit equals zero.

Hence in summary, we do not find Euler's theorem to be of much help in answering the question 'how are the distributive shares determined," especially under conditions of market imperfections. Within developing countries, the nature of the state, the extent to which trade unions are controlled by the state and the ruling political party, the development of markets and market processes are important factors in explaining the determination of distributive shares. If, for example, there are market distortions and shortages, then hawkers, traders and businessmen earn enormous rental incomes and so do public officials issuing licenses or rationing scarce goods. This scenario was experienced in Tanzania during the chronic shortages of the 1970s and 1980s, whether it was for basic consumer goods, textiles or building materials. Thus the determination of distributive shares in this case is best understood by taking into account the country's development strategy as well as the state of the economy in question.

Marginal productivity theory is necessarily based on the assumption of a given level of income in the economy as a whole. The crucial hypothesis of traditional marginal productivity theory is the assumption that consumer demand curves are invariant to the prices paid for the factors of production. Since the product demand curves are drawn up on the basis of fixed money incomes, marginal productivity analysis proceeds by treating the level of income as a datum.

The typical marginalist scheme of general equilibrium is a model of what has been known as a pure exchange economy (Pasinetti, 1981, 9). The model assumes the existence of given natural resources in fixed quantities and of a given number of individuals who own them. These individuals are further assumed to have well—defined utility functions. The problem is one of finding those equilibrium prices which bring about through exchange an optimum allocation of the given resources. Basically two types of goods exist: free goods, whose equilibrium prices are zero, and scarce goods, whose equilibrium prices are positive. The economic problem is then presented as being one of rational choice. Then it is argued that if these individuals behave rationally and act atomistically they will exchange among themselves the given commodities up to that point where the ratios of their

33

marginal utilities are equal to the corresponding price ratios. Not only will they have their utilities maximized at this point but no individual could become better off without some other individuals being made worse off (Pareto optimality). The Walrasian neoclassical theory is the archetype of general equilibrium theories. Within the Walrasian general competitive equilibrium the factor distribution of income depends on the nature of the production function(s), the supplies of the factor, the nature of utility preferences and the distribution of factor ownership among people with different utility preferences.

Application for African Growth:

The Marginal Productivity model is an extension of the Walrasian General Equilibrium model of supply and demand. In Africa, it's difficult to find equilibrium prices. The model works as a scholarly assessment but is flawed for an underdeveloped and emerging economy. Therefore, as an equilibrium model, we may conclude that Marginal Productivity will be practically irrelevant for use in African growth.

Keynesian Theories of Income Distrubution

1.   NICHOLAS KALDOR

Let P and W represent gross quasi—rent and aggregate wages respectively. Thus national income at factor cost is

$$Y \equiv P + W.$$

Kaldor assumes that the marginal (and average) propensities to save of capitalist (s_p) and workers (s_w) are given and constant and, in particular, that $s_p > s_w$. Total desired saving is

$$S = s_p P + s_w W,$$

and the aggregate desired saving ratio (s) is

$$s = \frac{S}{Y} = s_p \left(\frac{P}{Y} \right) + s_w \left(\frac{W}{Y} \right) = \left(s_p - s_w \right) \frac{P}{Y} + s_w.$$

Since saving must equal investment *ex post*, and since an equilibrium growth path requires *ex—ante* equality as well, Kaldor writes the above equation as follows:

$$s \equiv \frac{I}{Y} = \left(s_p - s_w\right)\frac{P}{Y}s_w.$$

$$\frac{I}{Y} = \overline{\left(\frac{I}{Y}\right)}$$

$$\frac{P}{Y} = -\frac{s_w}{\left(s_p - s_w\right)} + \frac{I}{\left(s_p - s_w\right)}\frac{I}{Y}$$

$$(2.5)$$

Solving equation (2.5) for the profit share, one obtains

$$\frac{P}{Y} = \frac{I}{\left(s_p - s_w\right)}\frac{I}{Y} - \frac{s_w}{\left(s_p - s_w\right)}$$

$$(2.6)$$

Equation (2.6) shows the profit share, and hence the share of labor, as depending upon the invest income ratio only, given the constant saving propensities. Since equation (2.6) is linear, its graphical counterpart is a straight line. The intercept is negative; and the slope is greater than unity since $o < s_p - s_w < I$ by hypothesis. Given the independently determined investment income ratio (I/Y),[1] the relative shares are automatically determined by mapping onto the ordinate.

The investment income theory of distribution is static, as may be seen from this formulation. However, to study the role of distribution in economic growth, Kaldor made a legitimate definitional substitution of terms; but after the substitution, the model has a misleadingly dynamic appearance. Note first that investment, by definition, is equal to the change in capital stock. Thus the investment income ratio may be written

$$\frac{I}{Y} = \frac{\Delta K}{Y}$$

$$(2.7)$$

Multiplying and dividing the right –hand side of equation (2.7) by ΔY, one obtains

35

$$s = \frac{S}{Y} = \frac{I}{Y} = \frac{\Delta Y}{Y}\frac{\Delta K}{\Delta Y}$$

(2.8)

Let us now consider equation (2.8). the first term on the right—most side, $\Delta Y/Y$, is the rate of growth of national income, denoted G. The second term, $\Delta K/\Delta Y$, is the marginal capital output ration or, in Harrod's terminology, the required capital output ratio (C_r). Consequently, equation (2.8) reduces to Harrod's famous equation for the warranted rate of growth:

$$G = \frac{s}{C_r}$$

(2.9)

Using equations (2.6) and (2.9), Kaldor argues that relative factor shares tend to be constant. Let G^w represent the warranted rate of growth and G^n the natural rate. Kaldor maintains that relative factor shares adjust so the $G^w = G^n$. but once so adjusted, there is no endogenous economic force to change them.

The adjustment mechanism may be explained as follows. Rewrite equation (2.9) as

$$G^w = \frac{s}{C_r} = \frac{\left(s_p - s_w\right)\left(P/Y\right) + s_w}{C_r}$$

(2.10)

In the absence of technological change, or if technological progress is Harrod neutral, C_r is a constant. Thus any change in G^w must come about through a change in the numerator. With given savings propensities, the change must come in P/Y.

s identities. From national income accounting relations, one obtains

$$Y \equiv P + W$$

(2.11)

Furthermore, using Kaldor's saving function,

$$S = s_p P - s_w W$$

$$(2.12)$$

The Kaldor equation relating the investment income ratio to the distribution of income may be derived from equations (2.11) and (2.12):

$$\frac{I}{Y} = (s_p - s_w) \frac{I}{1 + (W/P)} + s_w$$

$$(2.13)$$

Also, from accounting identities, an equation relating to distribution of income to the factor price ratio for any given labor capital ratio may be obtained:

$$\frac{W}{P} = \frac{P_l}{P_K} \frac{L}{K}$$

$$(2.14)$$

Equations (2.13) and (2.14) provide two equations in three unknowns, and no additional information can be obtained from accounting relations. Behavior equations, therefore, must supply the missing elements.

Let us turn first to an equation explaining the demand composition ratio. Given s_v and s_w, the average propensity to consume is $I - s_v (P/Y) - s_w (W/Y)$. Thus consumption ($= D_G$) is $Y - s_v P - s_w W$. Similarly, investment (D_I) is $s_v P + s_w W$. The ratio of consumption to investment (the demand composition ratio is accordingly,

$$\frac{D_G}{D_I} = \frac{(W/P) + I}{s_w (W/P) + s_p} - I$$

$$(2.15)$$

Since $s_v > s_w$ by assumption, equation (2.15) may be written more simply as:

$$\frac{D_G}{D_I} = f\left(\frac{W}{P}\right), \frac{df}{d(W/P)} > 0.$$

$$(2.16)$$

Equation (2.16) states that the demand composition ratio depends upon the distribution of income and that an increase in wages relative to profit causes an increase in the demand for consumer goods relative to investment goods.

What are the lessons to be learned from this? They are ones we already know.

1) This is a multi—commodity world in which different commodities require different factor combinations. Hence relative commodity demand must play some role in determining relative factor shares.

2) At the same time, as should be clear form the above model, useful analysis of the behavior of relative factor shares entails reference to the conditions of production. Hence production functions must also play an important role in the determination of relative factor shares.

At this stage it seems appropriate to indicate what the above model is and what it is not. It emphatically is not a theory of distributive shares. I hope that it is a vehicle for exposing the weaknesses of Kaldor's model.

In Kaldor's theory, investment is a completely exogenous variable whose behavior is not determined by the model. In fact, the Kaldor model simply determines the profit share that is consistent with full employment, given an exogenous level of investment and the unequal propensities to save. This is far from a theory of distribution. The force of this criticism is shown by an examination of Kaldor's solution in equation (2.6), which is obtained from (2.5) by simple algebraic operations. Equation (2.5) is an ex—post accounting identity, and equation (2.6) I must equal S, ex—ante and ex—post. There is no behavioral equation to explain investment; it simply must equal desired saving. Since P/Y depends upon the investment income ratio, there is also nothing in the model to explain distributive shares. P/Y is what it is because in equilibrium it is related to I/Y, and I/Y is what it is because it can be nothing else. Just as relative shares are technologically determined in neoclassical theory, so they are psychologically determined in Kaldor's theory, being ultimately determined by the propensities to save. As emphasized above, this is indeed a 'widow's curse' model of distribution and relative factor shares.

Application for African Growth:

Kaldor's model in general is unclear. He doesn't specify his variables 'y' and 's'. Are they prices or money? If they were well defined, we may find his assessment of capitalists and workers able to be more broadly and more realistically applied to multi—class societies. There is no reason why savings propensities should differ for various sources of income.

Kaldor is significant for situations where two classes are clearly distinguishable, however in Africa there are not only two classes. There are capitalists, there are workers, and there are peasants. Therefore, while Kaldor may seem attractive on the surface, he is not recommended for use in analyzing African economic activity.

2.   LUIGI PASINETTI

Pasinetti's well—known contribution (1962, 267—79) arose from the criticism which he advanced against Kaldor's model. Pasinetti redefined worker's income as including wages plus profits. Like Kaldor, he assumed that workers have a constant saving ratio, but this time a class propensity to save rather than propensity to save out of wages. In this model capitalists' propensity to save is larger than workers' propensity to save. The economy is assumed to be in a state of dynamic equilibrium, that is, he assumes a steady—state situation. The implications of the steady—state assumption are (1) all inputs and outputs have been growing at a steady rate since the beginning of time, with prices and the rate of interest constant, and (2) the factor distribution of income is constant.

Whence Pasinetti deduces that the shares of workers and capitalists in total capital, total profit and total savings are constant over time. Pasinetti's key assumptions are steady—state growth and constancy of the propensities to save. From his model:

The profit share is determined only by the aggregate investment ratio and the propensity of the capitalists to save, and

The rate of interest is independent of technology, that is, of any kind of production function.

Application for African Growth:

It can be argued that Pasinetti is not a realistic model for Africa. Technology is very important in the production process. Pasinetti argues that technology is independent of technology. But output is a function of technology and resources. You may not separate so conveniently as Pasinetti argued.

What Africa needs is a model that understands the vital role of technology in the generation of output.

3.   MICAHEL KALECKI

Historically, the first of the modern 'alternative' theories of distribution is Kalecki's, dating from 1938. And, it might be added, his theory is strongly influenced by the economic milieu of the 1930's. The theory in question, that is to say, gets its special character from Kalecki's observations of the industrial pricing process during the depression years.

Kalecki begins with the assumption that all firms always have excess plant capacity. In this situation, it is further assumed, output may be expanded by using additional units of labor and raw materials in about the same proportions as before. Thus marginal and average 'prime costs' per unit of output are approximately constant and, therefore, the marginal productivity curve is horizontal. Employment is determined by the level of output alone. At this point another distinctive feature of Kalecki's theory appears. He assumes a world of imperfect competition. Thus the output of each firm depends upon its own pricing policy, which Kalecki assumes to be a mark—up of prime costs. This assumed pricing policy, together with the assumptions that the number of workers and the wage bill are proportional to output, leads to Kalecki's chief conclusion: the share of wages in each firm's output is equal to the share of wage cost in the price of output.

Following Kalecki, the theory may be stated more precisely by using a bit of algebra. Let W denote the total wages paid to production workers and R be the amount spent on raw and processed material. Kalecki assumes that price is determined by applying a uniform mark—up to prime costs. Let k > I be the uniform amount by which prime costs are increased to obtain price. The gross value of the firm's output is accordingly $k(W + R)$. The margin over prime costs will of course be the greater the larger is k; and k is a measure of monopoly power.

Gross profit is $(k — I)(W + R)$ and gross value added, which is the sum of wages and gross profit, is $W + (k — I) (W + R)$. Hence the production worker share, denoted s, is

$$s = \frac{W}{W + (k - I)(W + R)},$$

or writing j for R/W,

$$s = \frac{I}{I + (k - I)(j - I)}. \qquad (2.16)$$

Kalecki focuses on mark—up pricing and rejected the perfect competition model as an explanation of prices and profits over the greater part of a modern industrialized economy.

Application for African Growth:
Some aspects of Kalecki's model are relevant in studying the price formation and income distribution in Africa. The character of market is an important determinant of the outcome of the economic process. In Africa, distortions, together with the dominant presence of monopolies in both marketing and distribution have affected incomes, thus leading to unfavorable income distribution.

4. HARROD – DOMAR

There have been three major surges in growth theory in this century. The first occurred I response to the work of Harrod (1939) and Domar (1946). The second surge was the so—called neoclassical response to the Harrod—Domar model. Solow 1959 was the most important trigger for his and there was an enormous outpouring of papers and books on the subject in the decade that followed. The third surge came from the works of Romer (1986) and Lucas (1988) and has given rise to what is called the theory of endogenous growth." Although, as Solow (1994) observes, it is still too early to fully evaluate it, endogenous growth theory is of considerable potential interest to the study of development because it attempts to address issues of importance to developing countries.

The original rise in interest in growth had little to do with underdevelopment. The works of both Harrod and Domar were essentially attempts to fill in the dynamic part of Keynesian macro—economics for capitalist economies. Yet the central message of the Harrod—Domar model has been used in developing economies to conceptualize the problem of development and to determine various targets for policy. It may, therefore, be useful to briefly sketch the Harrod—Domar model.

Consider a fixed—coefficient, constant—returns—to—scale production function,

$$Y_t = \min\{vK_t, bL_t\},$$

$$(2.17)$$

where Y_t is the total output of the economy and K_t and L_t are the aggregate amounts of capital and labor in the economy in period t; and v and b are fixed positive coefficients. If, for instance, $v = \frac{1}{4}$ (not an unrealistic number, when output and capital are both measured in real terms) and $b = 1$, then 4 units of capital and 1 unit of labor produce 1 unit of output (with no wastage of labor or capital).

To start with, let us consider a country which is overpopulated, so that min $\{vK_t, bL_t\} = vK_t$. Hence we could think of the production function as

$$Y_t = vK_t.$$

$$(2.18)$$

Here v represents the output—capital ratio in the economy, and $c \equiv 1/v$ is the more familiar capital—output ratio. If the capital stock increases by 1 unit, the annual output of the economy increases by v or $1/c$ units.

In this economy, let s be the marginal propensity to save and let us assume that whatever is saved gets invested. Let us, for simplicity, assume that capital depreciation is zero. Hence in period t, the increase in capital is equal to sY_t or svK_t.

Throughout this chapter, for a variable, X, that depends on time (such as Y_t, K_t or L_t), we shall use $\overset{.}{X}_t$ to denote the increase in X in period t. When dealing with continuous time and differentiable functions, $\overset{.}{X}_t$ will therefore denote

$\partial X(t)/\partial t$. And the growth rate of X will be denoted by $\hat{X}_t$. Thus $\hat{X}_t = \dot{X}_t / X(t)$. Hence what we have just derived is

$$\dot{K}_t = svK_t,$$

or
                                                                    (2.19)

$$\hat{K}_t = sv = \frac{s}{c}.$$

Because, by (2.18), income is proportional to capital in this model, it follows that

$$\hat{Y}_t = \frac{s}{c}.$$

                                                                    (2.20)

That is, the national income grows at a rate equal to the savings rate divided by the capital—output ratio.

This simple formula is famous and has been frequently invoked to justify certain policies in overpopulated less—developed countries. In the above example where $c = 4$, suppose the savings rate is 20 percent or $s = 0.2$. Hence we would expect such a country to grow at a rate equal to 1/20 or 5 percent. These numbers, in fact, approximately describe the Indian economy through the 1980's. Policy makers in India argued how India needed to increase its savings rate and make its capital more productive (that is, lower c), no doubt with an equation such as (2.20) in mind. Note further that, if population grows at a rate n, then per capita income will grow at a rate $(s/c) - n$.

Recall that the discussion thus far is valid only as long as we have no labor shortage. If n happens to be equal to s/c, then all is well; population, capital, and income grow at the same rate. If $n > s/c$, then there will be growing unemployment in the economy. What happens if?

As long as there is excess labor, capital and income will grow at the rate s/c, and unemployment will gradually vanish. When full employment is reached, the growth rate of income and capital will be constrained by the population growth rate. Hence, in the long—run equilibrium, $\hat{Y} = \hat{K} = n$. To establish this formally, note first that, once unemployment vanishes, $Y_t = bL_t$. Hence

$\hat{Y} = n, K_t = sY_t = sbL_t,$ and $\hat{K}_t = sbL_t / K_t.$ If $\hat{K}_t$ is constant, then L_t / K_t must be constant, and therefore $\hat{K} = n.$ It follows that in the "steady state," where all variables grow at constant rates per capita income remains unchanged. Note also that

$$\dot{K}_t = sY_t = s \min \{vK_t, bL_t\},$$

and therefore

$$\hat{K}_t = s \min \left\{ v, \frac{bL_t}{K_b} \right\}.$$

Hence

$$n = s \qquad \min \left\{ v, \frac{bL_t}{K_t} \right\}. \qquad (2.21)$$

But since $n < s/c \equiv sv$, it follows that $bL_t < vK_t$.

Hence, as is evident from (2.17), we can define these variables.

III. Agricultural Economics

THEORY OF THE PEASANT AGRICULTURAL ECONOMY

1. THE OPTIMIZING PEASANT

It has been fashionable to begin discussions of less developed economies by questioning one of the basic postulates of economic theory, namely, the assumption of economic rationality. There is little necessity for that ritual here. Field observations by respectable economists and the rapidity with which African peasant small—holders increased the production of various export crops, that were in great demand during the early post World War II period, provide a strong evidence for economic rationality of peasant farmer's. If any doubts are left, they have been seriously undermined by past econometric investigations both in Africa and elsewhere[4].

In general, each farmer is technically able to grow any of the crops commonly grown in his area, although the actual selection of crops vary slightly from farmer to farmer. One may therefore speak meaningfully of a "typical farmer". The farmer has fixed resource endowments, land, labor and technology. He is presumed for our purpose to produce on his own account, for it is well known that in the peasant economy of Kenya, with which we are primarily concerned, "individuals are normally entitled to the products of the soil, the results of their own labor and exertion, and there is no collective claim to these." Under these conditions an optimizing farmer would seek to maximize some objective function, which we may assume to be the total utility he derives from the product of his labor and the leisure he enjoys.

In pure subsistence, the farmer, isolated from the money economy and without the opportunity to trade, would grow no crops unless they were directly useful to him. For food crops, the maximum output he would desire would be that just sufficient to satisfy his consumption needs during the period in question and to provide seed where necessary, for the following season. A greater output would not increase utility from food consumption even though it would diminish his leisure.

Let us define the case of a farmer growing only one crop, a food crop. Defining the hours not devoted to agricultural production as "leisure"; the farmer thus has the following utility:

$$U = U(F, Lo) \qquad (3.1)$$

where **F** is the volume of food consumed(produced); and **Lo**, leisure. He maximizes his utility by putting just enough labor into agriculture to enable him to consume food at a level where the marginal utility of leisure of production equals the marginal utility to him. (It is assumed, of course, that second order conditions hold —— that is, that the second order derivative of **U** with respect to each argument is negative.)

Suppose a market now opens up so that this farmer has the opportunity to exchange some his food for another commodity that he does not produce. Let this commodity be homogeneous and divisible manufactured good, **R**, which cannot be produced on the farm with prevailing technology. Alternatively, **R** may be considered the farmer's real cash income, representing his generalized purchasing power in the monetary economy. If total food production is now denoted by **Q** and food sales for cash income by **S**, we have:

$$S = Q\text{-}F \tag{3.2}$$

If we take the price of the **R** good (money) as a numeraire, we may write:

$$R = P_1S \tag{3.3}$$

where P_1 is the exchange rate between **R** and **S**. How would our peasant farmer respond to a change in market price of food? Consider the following relations:

Total food supply
$$Q = Q(P_1) \tag{3.4}$$
Farmer's demand (consumption)
$$F = F(P_1) \tag{3.5}$$
Market supply of food
$$S = Q - F = S(P_1) \tag{3.6}$$

The farmer may be expected to respond to higher food prices by producing more food. That is, $Q'(P_1) > 0$. The farmer's utility function now has **R** as one of its arguments. Therefore, now that food is relatively expensive, he is likely to consume less food and more **R**, unless he, as a matter of principle, chooses to remain self—sufficient in food, in which case **F** will be invariant to changes in P_1. The increase in the price of food, of course, implies as an increase in the farmer's consumption of food, provided food is a normal or superior good, that is, his income elasticity of demand for food is positive. We assume that the substitution effect is stronger than the income effect. The above argument implies that:

$$F'/Q'<O \tag{3.7}$$
and
$$F'(P_1)<0 \tag{3.8}$$

We may also infer:

$$S'(P_1) = Q'(P_1) - F'(P_1)>Q'(P_1)>0$$
$$\tag{3.9}$$

Two conclusions emerge. If the farmer remains self—sufficient in food, that is, if $F'(P_1) = 0$, the supply curve for total food (production) has the same slope everywhere as the supply function for marketable surplus. If, however, the peasant farmer reduces the amount he consumes out of his own food production when the

46

price of food rises, that is, if $F'(P_1)<0$ (whether or not own produce is an inferior good), then the marketable surplus supply function is more elastic than the total food supply function.

If F is an inferior good it may only mean, of course, that as a farmer becomes more prosperous he consumes a wide variety of food "by importing food from the informal market." In this case he may simply improve the quality rather than increase the physical quantity of the food he consumes. On the other hand, F may remain constant so that in prosperity a farmer who purchases necessary food increases the quantity and possibly the quality of his total food consumption. Such a farmer's records, if he had any, would show him becoming increasingly dependent on purchased food for his subsistence needs. A farmer's dependence on purchased food may, however, be due to reasons other than prosperity, as we shall find later. It is therefore worthwhile to point out that if such growing dependence on purchased food is due to prosperity, the farmer's food basket should in prosperous times show increasing quantities and varieties of imported food from the formal market for which more or less perfect substitutes cannot be produced on the farm under prevailing circumstances.

Whatever the characteristics of F, a rational farmer would allocate his time in such a way as to produce enough food to enable him to consume at a point where the utility he derives from F and R are equal on the margin.

Now consider the case of a farmer producing two crops, food (F), which is not sold at all, and an export crop (T), which is not and cannot be consumed at all on the farm. The farmer produces the export crop only so he can exchange it for R. Again he allocates his resources in such a way as to consume a utility maximizing package R, F, leisure. He, in effect, directs into the production of T the labor that in the previous case went into the production of food for sale, S.

A more realistic and fruitful situation is one where our peasant farmer not only produces food for himself but also can earn his cash income by producing a marketable surplus food (S) or producing the export crop (T) or some combination of S, and T. Let P_2 be the exchange rate between R and T. The farmer's consumption of the manufactured good (his real cash income) is now determined by the following equation:

$$R = P_1 S + P_2 T \qquad\qquad (3.10)$$

Let L_a be the total labor input (measured in man—hours) in agriculture. The farmer is free to determine the size of L_a, the number of hours of work in agriculture, as well as how much L_a will go into each particular agricultural activity. We assume that he does his allocation with sole purpose of maximizing his utility.

This means on the one hand that he must choose to work that number of hours at which his marginal utility from work and his marginal utility from leisure (non—work) are equated.On the other hand, to maximize his utility from work, he must consume commodities now available to him as a result of work at levels where their marginal utilities are equal.

It may be supposed for simplicity that the farmer evaluates his total food output at going market price. When he consumes some of this food, it is because he buys it from himself by choice. His potential income—the total income he would realize if he were to sell his agricultural produce at going market prices—may be denoted by Y:

$$Y = P_1Q + P_2T \qquad (3.11)$$

Note that the above equation can be rewritten as:

$$Y = R + P_1F \qquad (3.12)$$

It is this value of his total product that the farmer maximizes in the first place, subject to the constraint of a given labor input, and then maximizes his total utility from work subject to his income constraint by allocating it appropriately.

Given the level of technology, the peasant farmer's production frontier is defined by the equation:

$$E\,(Q,T) = 0 \qquad (3.13)$$

For all nonnegative values of Q and T, there is one unique production frontier for each specified value L_a. In light of crop prices, maximizing the value of the farmer's total product subject to this technological constraint is equivalent to maximizing the lagrangean expression:

$$V_Q = P_1$$
$$E_Q = 0$$
$$V_T = P_2$$
$$E_T = 0$$

$$V = E(Q,T) = 0 \qquad (3.14)$$

Equations (3.14) imply

$$E_Q/E_T = P_1/P_2$$

From the latter it can be seen that the marginal rate of product transformation is

$$MRT_{QT} = —dT/dQ = P_1/P_2 \qquad (3.15)$$

Since from equation (3.12) it is obvious that the farmer should produce the combination of Q and T determined by the tangency of his iso—revenue function, Y, to his fixed product frontier. Note that for given crop prices and fixed technology, there is one and only one maximum value $Y^* = Y$. This is at the tangency mentioned above. It is the locus of Y^* corresponding to various values La that defines the terms of trade between leisure and income.

The marginal rate of substitution is measured by the magnitude of the slope of the isoquant. To calculate the marginal rate of technical substitution at point a is 2 and the farmer will produce good T rather than Q at point b. The farmer will choose good Q whereby good Q has marginal rate of substitution equal ½.

This terms of trade schedule is determined independently of the farmer's preferences and is obviously inversely related to leisure, since leisure is, by definition, non—work. The equilibrium values of leisure hours **(Lo)** and labor **(La)** are then determined by his preference map and the income—leisure terms of trade. This equilibrium point is attainable, however, only if the farmer allocates L_a efficiently among various crops he grows.

The analysis could be extended to cover a greater number of competing crops, but such analysis would not serve any useful purpose in the present context. There are no adequate time series data on individual crops, especially for individual farmers in Kenya. The primary reason, however, is that our central problem is the competition between food crops and export crops. In the present context it is assumed that there is only one crop in each category.

In this two—crop sector case, suppose that P_2, the price of **T** rises while P_1 the price of food does not. It means that the farmer can obtain **R** economically by selling **T** than by selling **S**. He would therefore increase his production of the export crop and reduce the production of the marketable surplus by reallocating his labor. But if the price of food itself has not fallen, the increase in P_2 implies an increase in the farmer's real income. On the account of the latter the farmer would like to increase his consumption of the home grown food, **F**, if homegrown food is a normal good. The expected total effect of a rise in the relative profitability of the export crop is a reduction in total food production, **Q**, and this reduction would be fully absorbed by marketed surplus, **S**. However, some of the reduction in total output would be reflected in a fall in **F**, the farmer's consumption of the home grown food, if the reduction in **Q** exceeds **S** or if the relative price changes are such that **F** becomes relatively more expensive than **R**.

It may be inferred that the farmer is indifferent between labor effort applied to **S** and that applied to **T**. One man—hour of farm work is just as "unpleasant" as another, regardless of the crop to which it is applied. The optimal combination of crops is not disturbed by the equi-proportionate changes in the profitability of the two crops. In general he will be satisfied with his time allocation only when the utility he ultimately derives from the last unit of effort applied to another activity.

In our case, he maximizes a utility function such as:

$$U = U(F,R) \qquad (3.16)$$

subject to the constraint defined by equation (3.11). It is easy to show that to do this he must satisfy the condition that the marginal rate of substitution **(MRS_FR)** of **F** for **R** equals P_1, the price of food. Thus;

$$MRS_{FR} = U_F/U_R = P_1 \qquad (3.17)$$

Equations (3.15) and (3.17) above yields the relationship below:

$$P_1 = MRS_{FR} = MRT_{QT}.P_2 \qquad (3.18)$$

The latter condition is satisfied whenever the farmer is in equilibrium both as a producer and as a consumer.

Continual improvements in the relative profitability of **T** vis—a—vis **Q**—that is, a rise in P_2 relative to P_1 would thus lead the farmer to shift production continually in favor of **T**, until MRT_{QT} falls sufficiently to restore equation (3.18), first in production equation (3.15) and then, if necessary, in consumption equation (3.15). Conversely, if over time the production of **T** has increased relative to the production of food, given fixed resources and technology, we may infer that the profitability of **Q**, provided the farmer's resources can be transferred in either direction with equal facility.[5]

2. IMPACT OF EXPORT CROP EXPANSION

If production of **T** increases then either **Q** has gone down or the production frontier has shifted outward. This is so because technology is fixed and only labor must have increased in agriculture. Is it realistic to expect the rise in **T** to be at the expense of **Q**— that is, at the expense of **F** or **S**? There are at least three possible situations in which an affirmative answer is suggested.

For a peasant farmer producing a marketable food surplus as well as export crop for cash, there is no reason to expect an increase in marginal revenue in food crops to be different from similar increase in export crop. For such a farmer, a substitution of **T** for **Q** on the margin may realistically be expected when the relative prices of **T** rises.

Assuming that the farmer's production set is convex, we can say that, in terms of food export crops expansion is cheaper for a peasant farmer just beginning commercial production than for one for whom production for export has become commercial activity. This is because the marginal rate of product transformation between food crops and export crops falls as export crop production increases. Such a farmer may be able to substitute **T** production for food crops in the early stages of commercial activity because he may be restricted to consuming what he produces and consumes them in excess of subsistence and consequently his marginal utility is small.

Finally, a farmer may willingly substitute **T** for food production regardless of his initial level of food production if there is a market where he can purchase food with some of his income, provided this substitution increases total utility.

But suppose the farmer places a premium on the production on the food he consumes, due to some reason or other he does not trust the market to satisfy his needs as a food buyer. This is probably unique to developing economies. In that case, as his total food production, **Q**, approaches his own consumption requirements, **F**, he may become less responsive to the increases in the relative profitability of **T**. If there is some level of **Q**, say Qo = Fo, below which he does not want to reduce food production we have:

$$MRT\ >P_1/P_2\ \text{when}\ Q = 0 \qquad (3.19)$$

In this case, the farmer maximizes the value of total output subject to a technological constraint in equation (3.19), as well as to a known food consumption constraint, **Q>Fo.**

The farmer's desired minimum level of food production may be socially defined or otherwise subjectively determined. It probably increases with his real income[6]. Somewhere plausibly below it but certainly not above it, is the minimum subsistence consumption level that the farmer must maintain in order to live. We may call the desired minimum food production the farmer's reservation price or transfer income in export crop production since it is the minimum amount of food he must be assured of consuming from proceeds of his export crop sales in order to induce him to give up food production in favor of agricultural export production. Actual food consumption, even from own production alone, may well exceed this reservation demand, particularly in good crop years.

What factors would cause a farmer to place a premium on food production and thus determine the size of his reservation price? In a community of largely self—sufficient farmers, food is not always available in the total market though this constraint should change as the economy becomes more developed. The farmer who does not produce food may therefore have to obtain it elsewhere – perhaps from the nearest town or another village. This entails relatively high transportation costs, which raises the farmer's buying price of food even if actual market prices of food have not changed appreciably. He may also fear that other farmers will shift into export crop production and that the resulting reduction in aggregate food production would cause food prices to rise even further. The price he expects to pay for food is therefore invariably higher than the prevailing market prices and the prices at which he expects to sell.

It may be also be the farmer's income from either crop alone is more unstable than that from some combinations of both crops, regardless of whether this instability is of supply or demand origin. In that event, although his expected income from specialization may be higher than the reservation price, while the lowest possible incomes from specialization may be to starve in bad years if the capital market is so imperfect that he in effect has no access to credit. Such a farmer may diversify by growing both crops simply in order to minimize the danger in bad years[7]

Whatever the reasons may be, it is a well—documented fact that peasant farmers do place a high premium on self—sufficiency in food. The underlying explanation seems to be that risk aversion increases greatly when a farmer's food production is close to his biological subsistence level. A farmer may therefore be quite rational in having no desire to specialize in export crop production even if his expected income from such specialization would be higher.

The reluctance to specialize in export production may be even stronger where the export crop is a tree crop, which, because of its perennial nature, makes decisions irreversible for long periods of time. If the export crop were an annual crop, the farmer might be less hesitant because his production decisions could be completely revised every year. The farmer will therefore wait until he is fairly convinced that the increase in the relative profitability of the export crop is more or less permanent before tying up his land with an export tree crop. This special effect of a tree crop is relevant, however, only where land is an effective constraint on production. Where land is in surplus supply, the farmer could "abandon" the tree crop farm in bad export crop years and return to it in good years, assuming that temporary abandonment does not affect future tree crop yields too adversely.

A farmer may also be reluctant to specialize in food production even he appears to have comparative advantage in food, fearing that other farmers may specialize in food too. Because of the small size of the internal market, food prices and income tend to fall when there is good harvest. A rigorous specification of the nature of uncertainty faced by the peasant farmer is not necessary in order to reach this conclusion. An empirical estimation to show that export crop production has been at the expense of food crop is required. It remains to ascertain empirically whether this expansion has in fact been achieved because the typical farmer has moved along his production frontier, or because he has somehow managed to shift his production frontier outward.

3.   INTER—SECTOR TRADE LINKS

In order to examine further effects of the expansion of nonfood crops, it is useful to regard agricultural economy as consisting of three sectors, each producing only one product, and to introduce the non—agricultural sector or the modern sector as the fourth sector of the national economy. Let I be the food in the formal sector; II, the agricultural export sector, III, food crops in the informal sector; and IV, the modern sector. Suppose all the sectors trade with each other and that each sector sells only its own product to other sector of the economy. Let X_{ij} denote the volume of sales from sector i to j. The intersectoral trade flows are shown in the following matrix.

TABLE 3.1   **Agricultural Economic Sectors**

Source	Destina-tion	I	II	III	IV
F_F	I	X_{11}	X_{12}	X_{13}	X_{14}
F_I	II	X_{12}	X_{22}	X_{23}	X_{24}
Q_E	III	X_{31}	X_{32}	X_{33}	X_{34}
U_s	IV	X_{41}	X_{42}	X_{43}	X_{44}

Source: Compiled by Author

The total domestic production of food is the sum of the first and second row:

$$X_1 = X_{ij} \qquad (3.20)$$

It is important to note that X_{21}, X_{22}, X_{23} are identical to zero in the case of pure export crops. In that case the entire export produce is sold to the urban sector, for export. Where the three sectors in agriculture consist of distinctly different persons, sectors II and III consumers pay for their food purchases from sector I by maintaining a trade surplus with sector IV.

4.   CONCLUSION

The literature reviewed in sections 1 through 3 did not show an analysis of how to alleviate poverty in Kenya, but rather showed us how the rural farmer in Kenya makes economic decisions in terms of resource allocation; this is the condition that a Kenyan peasant farmer actually faces. The link between the above literature and poverty was not addressed. In chapter four, we will present and assess two models that extend the analysis to show how an overall increase in agricultural output can reduce poverty in Kenya. This will be explored in two ways: first, with a general linear model where poverty is a dependent variable; and second, with an alternative model which maximizes nominal income thus reducing poverty. The minimization of poverty, therefore, is equivalent to the maximization of net nominal income. Our problem consists of determining the net nominal income which will be maximized. For now then, let's look at how the facts of rural life in Kenya justify the economic theories of the optimizing peasant as we've just discussed.

Structure of the Rural Economy

We shall describe some aspects of rural economic structure that have emerged from the field survey, in order to provide a basis to what assumptions underlie the econometric and the alternative mathematical models in chapter four, "A Conceptualized Framework". In particular, we shall be concerned with the relative importance of various crops, the market orientation of farmers, the constraints on production and the degree of diversification in production. The analysis should provide a useful background for evaluating the preceding theoretical analysis and for assessing the focus of the chapters that follow in terms of poverty alleviation.

A number of criteria could be used to rank the importance of different crops. Among these are the crops' contribution to total farm incomes, their contribution to total food consumption and the number of farmers growing each crop. Each of these criteria will be analyzed below. In each case, it will be shown that the proportion of farmers growing a given crop is generally a useful indicator of the relative importance of that crop to the economy.

TABLE 3.2   **Relative Importance of Various Crops**

Crop	Contribution to Total Farm Income %	Contribution to Food Consumption %	Number of Farmers Growing %
Maize	90	95	100
Milk	95	50	100
Coffee	49	—	50
Tea	40	—	55
Pyrethrum	15	—	25
Millet	20	50	40
Vegetables	10	50	29
Wheat	45	25	30
Meats	30	45	25
Potatoes	5	20	20

Source: Compiled by Author

In order to elicit the required information, farmers in each sample were confronted with a fairly exhaustive list of crops that were known to be grown in some parts of the country. This confrontation with a list is superior to total reliance on farmers' recall, for, in general, such recall when unaided, tends to be incomplete.

Before we proceeded with the results, some mention should perhaps be made of communication weakness that were discovered and corrected during the pre—testing in order to increase the reliability of the answers. The first concerns the time reference of the respondents. It is not uncommon for a farmer to say he grows a particular crop if he once grew it but for some reason or other has given it up. It was thus necessary to ask each farmer if he was currently growing the crop or had grown it in during the previous year. Only the farmers who answered the latter question in the affirmative were regarded as growing that crop. Secondly, farmers generally associated the phrase "growing a crop" with the processing or planting. A farmer might say he does not grow tea or coffee if he had not brought any new acreage under these crops recently. The possibility of such misleading answers was eliminated by asking each farmer first whether he grew the crop; if his answer was negative, he was the asked if he had harvested any of that crop during the time period in question.

The results are shown on Table 3.5 above. These results can be used to classify crops according to their relative importance by percentage of total farmers growing them. The following chart depicts the results of the classification of crops.

The chart shows that for the country as a whole, the most widespread food crops by far are maize, vegetables, beans and milk. It is worth noting that most maize areas a have wider range of major crops than other areas.

Some assessment of the representativeness of our ranking can be made by comparing the conclusion of our figures with those of Kenyan statistical abstracts. This is depicted in Table 3.5 above.

Both sets of data clearly demonstrate the same trend for all four crops to be the most important food crops, with maize having an edge over the other two, while bananas in fourth place are of considerably less importance. The differences in the magnitudes of two sets of data are of no great consequences especially since the official statistics fluctuate over a wide range in a short period of only three years. What is important to note is that the primacy of these three crops is validated by what is generally known from other sources in reference both to rural diets and to total acreage under various crops.[8]

1.   MARKET AND SUBSISTENCE ORIENTATION

Price and other monetary incentives have their main direct impact on economic agents who are in the money economy, although these incentives also influence the rate of entry into the money economy. The effectiveness of such policies in agriculture thus depends heavily on the degree to which growers of particular crops are in the exchange economy. Ideally the degree of market orientation of individual farmers and the peasant sector as a whole should be measured in terms of the proportion of total farm output that is sold. Where land under crops is fairly evenly distributed among farmers, the degree to which population is market—oriented will reasonably reflect the extent to which cultivated land is devoted to production for the market. In western Kenya, 89 percent of all farmers held 71 percent of total land under crops in 1996; their farm sizes ranged from half an acre to less than five acres.

TABLE 3.3   **Percentages of Sample Farmers Growing Various Crops**

Crops	Nandi	Keri-cho	Uasin Gishu	Keiyo	Bar-ingo	Tran-zoia	All Areas
Maize	100	100	100	90	70	100	93
Sugar	20	25	—	—	—	5	8
Wheat	25	5	50	40	45	70	45
Coffee	30	10	—	2	5	35	20
Tea	40	60	—	5	2	25	38
Millet	50	70	5	25	75	68	60
Vegeta-bles	20	45	4	5	5	23	38
Potatoes	25	40	40	35	45	32	36
Pyre-thrum	15	10	55	45	30	43.4	24
Sorghum	10	45	7	60	75	62	30
Oats	—	5	20	10	2	73	15
Dairy	100	100	90	90	90	71	91

Source: Compiled by the Author.

Turning to the food crops, we find an entirely different picture. Production becomes more of a subsistence activity, aimed primarily at directly satisfying on—farm demand. Over 80 percent of farmers of major food crops sell less than half of their product. Nearly 90 percent of farmers growing beans and vegetables belong to this class; in fact, some 75 percent of all farmers and two thirds of the bean growers sell none at all of their produce. These results are shown in Table 3.7 below.

To view the results from another angle, we see that with the exception of cassava and rice (which is not an important crop in Kenya), less than 5 percent of all farmers sell all of any food crop they grow. The subsistence orientation of beans is particularly interesting when it is recalled that beans are probably the most important food crop in the internal trade of Kenya.

The relatively heavy market orientation of some food crops calls for some discussions. In case of cassava, the reason seems to be that the crop requires considerable processing before it is ready for consumption. Many of the farmers explained that they sold their cassava raw and often still standing in the field because they did not know how to process it. Such farmers bought the processed cassava products, such as gari and cassava flour, which they themselves consumed. This was particularly the case with the bachelors and other farmers who did not have their wives living with them in the village. They might well have explained quite correctly, although surprisingly enough they did not, that processing cassava is considered a woman's chores.

Wheat is grown primarily for sale only in the urban centers. Strategically located between the two major centers of Nairobi and Mombasa, 26 percent of farmers sell more than half of their wheat output.

TABLE 3.4   **Market Orientation of Farmers by Percentage of Output Sold Rift Valley Province**

	Percentage of Total Growers Reporting				Total Grow-ers
	None Sold	Less Than Half Sold	More Than Half Sold	All Sold	
Coffee	10.0	—	—	96	108
Tea	18.8	8.3	—	98	180
Pyre-thrum	53.3	6.7	—	89	45
Maize	15.4	20.0	45	70	16
Oats	46.2	34	12	78	13
Vegeta-bles	54.5	24	8	80	56
Millet	65.5	56	11	65	145
Wheat	42.2	50	—	81	60
Dairy	13.5	90	—	100	200
Potatoes	30.8	29	19	70	86
Pineap-ples	56.7	—	35	68	60
Poultry	51.4	5	16	90	189
Wool	53.2	—	26	97	8
Fruits	36.9	—	12	80	12

Source: Compiled by Author

Thus the aggregates tend to obscure certain important differences among areas. One other example is maize, which is the most important cash crop in the rift valley province despite heavy subsistence orientation in most parts of the country. In this savanna country, which is ecologically unsuited for rice, 75 percent of the farmers growing maize sell more than half of their entire product. Pyrethrum is also an important cash earner in the Rift valley province. But the Pyrethrum Board of Kenya, which decides who should grow the crop and how much is to be grown by each grower, largely controls production. As a virtual monopoly, it enforces its control by buying only the assigned quota from each approved grower and none at all from other growers. Only the latter growers, who sold their crop in the local market, were included in our sample. The reason was that since entry into pyrethrum cultivation is controlled, the proportion of farmers growing pyrethrum and the relative importance of pyrethrum on their farms would not be fair reflection of the outcome of the farmers' own decisions.

We earlier suggested that it may be reasonable to assume in Kenya that the proportion of farmers selling their produce in any class bears a high positive correlation to the proportion of their total output which is sold. This is shown in Table 3.7 above. If this assumption is valid, food production in the eastern Rift valley is heavily oriented toward subsistence, particularly in coffee growing areas where certain amount of specialization in export production has taken place. In the areas where coffee is of little or no importance, at least one food crop has become a "cash crop" in the sense that it is grown primarily for sale.

2.   CONSTRAINTS ON PRODUCTION

At any point in time, growth in agricultural output in Kenya can be explained primarily in terms of inputs of land and labor only. The overwhelming bulk of production takes place in "traditional fashion," without the use of mechanical or, frequently animal power. Rainfall is generally adequate in quantity and reliability so that irrigation is unnecessary and thus unknown to the farmers. Yet farmers frequently complain about a shortage of capital with which to do their work. Most farmers in all the villages visited considered that the most important problem faced by the people of their village was capital/money.

Before discussing the effectiveness of this constraint, it may be useful to consider its nature. We found that traditional Kenyan agriculture uses practically no inputs from outside the agricultural sector. The major exception is coffee, for which spraying is a regular practice. The amount of spraying done, however, depends on total coffee acreage, which itself is determined by the amount of land and labor available. Cash is therefore primarily a means of acquiring more land or, more often, additional labor. In most instances, capital is no more than a "subsistence fund" that the farmer needs in order to maintain his family and laborers during the months when his crops are not yielding revenue.

Each farmer was asked why in the current year he had not planted more of each of a number of the major crops of the area. He was asked if the most important reason was included in our list of suggested possibilities, and, if not, to give his own reasons (see APPENDIX B). Responses of "that was all I could maintain" and " insufficient labor" were added together as a measure of a labor shortage.

Table 3.8 shows the distribution of the responses for coffee. Both land and labor appear to be effective constraints on production. Suitable coffee land seems to be the most single bottleneck, and it is relatively more serious in older coffee areas. Labor is scarce because it commands a positive price in the free market, and also many farmers depend on hired labor for crop expansion. Hired labor from the relatively labor abundant areas of the country is, however, usually available at the going wage rate. Labor therefore becomes an effective constraint only when the marginal revenue of agricultural output is at such a low level that it is un economic to increase output by hiring more labor. Often this labor shortage would reflect itself as capital shortage when willing farmers lack the financial resources with which to hire laborers and do not have access to credit facilities.

For food crops land becomes less important as a constraint as can be seen from Table 3.8. It is clearly less restrictive in the non—coffee areas and is, in fact, not a constraint at all in the Rift Valley area of Kericho.

Some of the Author's experiences in the field are worth relating here. In Runyenjes division of Meru district, farmers who had initially been in a hurry to go to their farms, volunteered a forty—five minute discussion of their credit problems at the end of the formal interviews. They wanted the government to be informed that one of their most desperate needs was an efficient credit system that would enable them to employ more laborers during their peak months.

TABLE 3.5   **Distribution of Respondents Citing Various Constraints on Coffee and Tea Production**

Labor	Land	Capital	Credit	Other
25%	45%	75%	95%	20%

Source: Compiled by Author

In Rift Valley Province, farmers testified that there was plenty of uncultivated land. This land is available for agricultural use or surplus land. How can the two pieces of evidence be reconciled? What are farmers really complaining about when they complain about a land shortage?

A possible explanation may be the land tenure system. Land in most parts of Kenya belongs to the old males. Ethnic group, the village, and/or the family—and individuals cannot usually alienate or acquire land through the market process. It has therefore been suggested that some farmers, confined to their meager family holdings, may be starved for land while others are burdened with excess land that cannot or will not be put to profitable use but cannot be sold to the needy farmers. This view, however, takes too static view of traditional land tenure and seriously undermined by pieces of evidence put together by other observers.

The writer is unaware of any instances when a Kenyan was prevented from being a farmer because he could not have access to land. Unallocated land is generally allocated quite automatically by the village chief to needy farmers who asked for it, and where no such land exists, these farmers can usually acquire land by leasing it or borrowing it from land rich families. Quite often the land is held in perpetuity by the grantee, and the "grantee can do virtually what he likes with the land short of alienating it to strangers or selling it to strangers or selling it."

Nor does the tenure system necessarily imply insecurity of tenure system, which may be deterrent to long—range planning. "Land once granted by a chief is to all intents and purposes beyond his care, so long as the grantee does not break any important condition of his occupancy." And even an offending farmer does not stand to loose all the future income streams arising from his investments.

It is also argued that "stranger" (immigrant) farmers are restricted as to the kinds of crops they can grow, that they are usually prevented from growing permanent (tree) crops. It is not known how widespread or restrictive this practice is. What is known is that in the coffee and tea areas there are many immigrants from other areas who depend heavily on wage income from employment in these industries.

Finally, it may be added that even if immigrant farmers were restricted to food crops, it would only result in their specialization in food production while the indigenous population would then become more specialized in export production. Such specialization would not be a constraint on agricultural production. The fact that the individual cannot alienate his land might adversely affect agriculture since the land cannot be used as collateral for agricultural loans, although his freedom to pledge his crops extenuates the situation to some extent. But this is entirely different matter from that of a land shortage. We must therefore seek other explanations for the complaints about a land shortage.

In the first place, coffee and tea farmers, as we observed earlier, devote a substantial share of their land to food production. It would thus be possible for farmers to increase their export acreage by replacing some of their food farms with export production and buying more of their food needs if export crops were sufficiently profitable to justify such specialization.

In the second place, most farmers said that they could increase their export acreage if export crop prices were to rise substantially. Asked where they would find the necessary land they answered that there was plenty of land "far away," which they could utilize if rewards for their efforts (in terms of the price of exports) were high enough to make it worth their while. In other words, cultivating distant plots of land entails transportation costs that must be covered by the product price before the farmer will regard such plots as available and useful. Although no money is involved for these farmers, transportation costs are real to farmers who have to trudge through difficult and dew drenched footpaths in order to reach their farms. We are led to conclude that how far farmers are willing to travel from village to farm depends directly on the pressure on land (population density) and on the profitability of their crops. In such context, given the population density and the real prices of agricultural produce, farmers could testify to a land shortage even if there exists uncultivated land that they could freely bring under crops.

Discussions with some of the older farmers suggested the following hypothesis about how the system operates. When population increases or there is a sustained increase in the demand for agricultural produce, farmers will travel longer distances to establish farms.

3. DIVERSIFICATION OF PRODUCTION

The discussion of the relative importance of various crops suggests that there is substantial crop diversification by farmers all over Rift Valley. What is the nature of this diversification, and how widespread is it? Farmers may be diversified in the sense that they produce for more than one market or for both domestic and export market or they may be diversified in the sense that each farmer grows more than one crop. The incidence of both types of diversification was investigated and will now be discussed.

Table 3.9 indicates that for the province as a whole 70 percent of all farmers grow both food crops and non—food crops. The degree of diversification (proportion of total farmers who are diversified) by area is positively associated with intensity of export crops (proportion of export crop farmers to total farmers). Conversely, the less important that export is in an area, the more likely that area's farmers will specialize fully in food production. Nearly everywhere we investigated showed that all farmers specialize in food production almost 90 percent of the time.

Measured by the number of crops grown by each farmer, the intensity of diversification becomes even more impressive. This is illustrated in Table 3.7, which shows that rarely does a farmer grows just one or two crops, no matter what his crop may be. Over 88 percent of the farmers sampled grew four or more different types of crops every year. The figure varies from a low of 77 percent in Keiyo to high 97 percent in Kericho. Outside Uasin Gishu the farmer more typically grows six or more different types of crops.

TABLE 3.6   Diversification: Percentage of Farmers growing both Food
Crops and Non—food Crops

Area	Both Food Crops and Non—Food Crops		Specialized	Total Farmers	
	Number	% of Total	Number of Total	Number	% of Total
Kericho	28	65.1	15	63	100
Nandi	31	100.1	10	49	100
Keiyo	27	100.0	7	80	100
Uasin Gishu	30	90.9	3	78	100
Tranzoia	4	10.8	56	57	100
Baringo	30	15.0	60	37	100
All Areas	120	70.2	25.8	25	100

Source: Compiled by Author

A number of reasons could be suggested as possible explanations for this high degree of diversification. The most important is probably the premium that farmers place on self sufficiency in food. This is due in part to the small size of rural markets and the unreliability of rural market supplies of foodstuffs. Another factor may be farmer's desire to minimize fluctuations in their incomes. Even if all crops were equally subject to the effects of changing weather conditions, variations in the prices of food crops and export crops might be independent of each other because of the probable independence between the internal market and external market (export) market. Thus, even when diversification in the same geographical area is powerless against supply—induced fluctuations, it may effectively reduce income instability of demand origin. In fact, a number of crops vary considerably in their sensitivity of timing, amount, and distribution of rainfall. For instance, millet is resistant to drought, whereas tea and coffee are very sensitive to it. Accordingly, even supply—induced fluctuations may be effectively tempered by diversification. The explanations given by farmers themselves are not very sophisticated, but they are suggestive and may be of interest to the reader.

These explanations, revealing a high premium on self—sufficient in food, are consistent with the theoretical analysis of the peasant agricultural economy detailed in the literature review. Asked why he was growing food crops instead of specializing, one farmer replied that a farmer wouldn't forget food crops just because of tea or coffee. A third farmer expressed the same sentiment more dramatically: "If you don't grow food crops, you will die of hunger."

A detailed examination of the causes of diversification does not belong here. It will suffice for now to say that much potential still exists for specialization and its attendant increases in the aggregate agricultural product without any major changes in farm techniques and practices.

TABLE 3.7 **Diversification: Distribution of Farmers by Number of Crops Grown**

Number of Crops Grown	Kericho		Nandi		Baringo		Uasin Gishu		Tranzoia		All Areas	
	No.	% of Total	No.	% of Total	No.	% of Total	No.	% of Total	No.	% of Total	No.	% of Total
One	—	—	—	—	—	—	1	2.9	1	2.7	2	1.2
Two	—	—	—	3.4	2	6.7	—	—	1	2.7	4	2.3
Three	4	9.5	2	6.9	1	3.3	—	—	7	18.9	14	8.1
Four or Five	12	28.6	12	41.4	10	33.3	5	14.3	18	48.6	57	32.9
Six or More	26	61.9	14	48.3	17	56.7	29	82.9	10	27.0	96	55.5
Total Farmers	42	100.0	29	100.0	30	100.0	35	100.0	37	100.0	100	100.0

Source: Compiled by Author

We have seen that farmers in Kenya exist only partially within the monetary economy. For a large number of them food production is a pure subsistence activity aimed at directly satisfying the food requirements of the producer. In such a setting, monetary incentives alone may be quite weak in their effectiveness. In this setting farmers are likely to place a high premium on self—sufficiency in food as a result of numerous factors discussed in the literature on the theory of the optimizing peasant.

Finally, our assumption that farmers are highly diversified is validated by the findings discussed in this chapter. The opportunity for specialization and its potential benefits are still very considerable and could be the source of substantial increases in total agricultural production even without major changes in the present level of technology.

CONCLUSION

The conclusion of the preceding analysis has shown us the significance of agricultural output for African economies. Food growth and export crops are the backbone of the agricultural economy. And the agricultural economy itself is the spinal chord of alleviating poverty in sub-Saharan Africa. In order to know how to increase output, we have to analyze determinants of poverty, for which we have developed the econometric model. And that is the subject of the next chapter.

IV. CONCEPTUALIZED FRAMEWORK OF POVERTY IN AGRICULTURE

This research study will analyze these causes of poverty using the following model. This model identifies the structural characteristics prevalent in a small open country economy. International price of exports and imports, which influence the rural household income, are exogenously determined whereas domestic producer prices are affected both exogenously and endogenously by:

A)   Foreign demand of agricultural products.

B)   Rate of surplus extraction by the government.

The study will be analyzed empirically by use of an econometric model[ix] of agricultural output and poverty alleviation applicable to Kenya.

Structural Characteristics of the Model

This model has the following five distinctive structural characteristics:

A)   The size and composition of agricultural production are a function of the various relative prices and investment in agricultural sector.

B)   Investment in agricultural sector is largely influenced by the patterns of government expenditure in agricultural sector.

C)   International trade represents a large portion of Kenya's GNP, and agriculture in such trade is quite large.

D)   Price focus analysis whereby Kenya is a price taker and thus Kenya's agricultural exports don't influence international agricultural prices.

E)   Given the fourth assumption by and large, increase in Kenya's exports should not have an adverse effect on Kenya's real incomes.

F)   Finally, given that the economy is open, market clears, and price taker assumption then it is compatible with the Walrasian assumptions of general equilibrium.

Objectives of the Model

Given the above structural characteristics, international terms of trade can thus be assumed. These terms of trade are a significant determinant of Kenya's real incomes as well as of the size and composition of agricultural production. Given the need for increased agricultural output, the following achievements must be realized:

A)   Increased technological change in the food crop sector which would lead to a release of resources for export crop production

B)   Increased technological change in the export crop sector that would result in an increase in import capacity.

C)   The domestic price is influenced by international terms of trade and the extent of net extraction by the government. The latter influences levels of poverty through its effect on both prices and public investment, which in turn can determine levels of agricultural output and avert market failures through investments transport infrastructure, which increases factor and product mobility. The relative importance to be attached to technological change and other investments in two sectors should depend on marginal returns to investments in particular crops.

Model Specification

This study on poverty will be analyzed using the following model. This model emphasizes that the size of agricultural production and the level of prices act as the determinants of the population living below the poverty line.[x] The dissertation has identified the structural characteristics of the small open agricultural economy. Through a simple model, the study outlines the role of international and domestic terms of trade and the size of agricultural production in influencing the incidence of poverty in Kenya, arguing that the major determinants of Kenyan rural poverty are the size of overall agricultural tradable commodities relative to prices of imports, and the domestic producer price of food and export crops. The size and composition of agricultural production are a function of the various relative prices and investment in the agricultural sector. Investment in agriculture is largely influenced by the pattern of government expenditures in the agricultural sector. In Kenya agriculture contributes more than 60 percent of the GNP. It is the public expenditure patterns that determine the extent which these revenues extracted by the government from the agricultural sector are siphoned back to agriculture for future agricultural production.

1.   **THE BASIC MODEL**

The general linear model can be estimated as follows[xi]

$$\mathbf{Pov} = \alpha + \beta_0 \mathbf{Y_R} + \beta_1 \mathbf{P_{ff}} + \beta_3 \mathbf{GR} + \upsilon \qquad (4.1)$$

Where: **Pov** = poverty

         $\propto$ = constant

         $\mathbf{Y_R}$ = agricultural household income

         $\mathbf{P_{Ff}}$ = price of food

         GR = government expenditures on agricultural public investments

         u = error term

The model nominal rural income:

$$Y_R = P_F Q_F + S_B + S_S + R \qquad (4.2)$$

Where:

Y_R = rural household income
P_F = producer prices of agricultural commodities
S_B = subsidies received by the agricultural sector
S_S = subsidies received by the agricultural sector
R = remittance of rural workers working in non agricultural sector
Q_F = quantities of agricultural commodities

Assumptions of the Equation [4.2]:

(1) rural sector = agricultural sector
(2) urban sector = public sector
(3) income received in form of subsidies on agricultural inputs (S_b), food supplies or other factors entering into rural production or consumption is negligible.

Agricultural household income:

$$Y_R = P_{Ff} Q_{Ff} + P_E Q_E \qquad (4.3)$$

Where:
P_{Ff} = nominal producer prices of food crops in the formal market
P_E = producer of export crops in the formal market
Q_{Ff} = quantities of food crops sold in the formal market
Q_E = quantities of export crops

2. POVERTY IN SUBSISTENCE AGRICULTURE

Certain areas of Kenyan rural sector are completely subsistence[xii] oriented where export crop production is constrained by physical resource endowment of land.
Thus: $Q_E = 0$
Economic implications of the above equation:
(1) Increase in food crop production should lead to increase in food available for household consumption. This implies a direct relationship between food production and poverty reduction.

(2) There exists an unknown condition of the above implication whether it would increase household income. This would depend on the behavior of the formal market prices, (P_{Ff}).

3.   GOVERNMENT AS A SURPLUS EXTRACTOR

The terms of trade and benefits to producers, depends on the rate of surplus extraction by the government and patterns of public expenditures[xiii]. Therefore, the government acts as intermediary in influencing the domestic terms of trade.

Now let: $P_{Ff} = P_C - M_C$ (4.4)

Where: P_C = official price of food
              M_C = marketing cost of the government agency

The government is a monopsonist in urban sale of food, therefore:
              P_C = exogenous government monopoly purchase of food crop

and $M_C = M_T + G$ (4.5)

Where: M_T = transport costs of buying food from rural pro ducers
              G = amount extracted by the government

and $G = A_C + T_A$ (4.6)

Where: A_C = administrative costs of parastatals
              T_A = the tax imposed on the rural sector

The size of G in this case may be exogenously determined by large administrative costs which may be used by the government for the investment projects. Also government acts as a monopsonist in the purchase of export crops either directly or indirectly through the publicly sponsored cooperatives. Thus:

$$M_T = f(T, F, S)   (4.7)$$

Where: T = amount of transport, equipment and spares
              M_T = internal transportation costs of the formal mar ket
              F = fuel imported by the government through admin istrative fiat

$$S = \text{stock of transport equipment imported}$$

The total amount of transportation equipment and spares (**T**) imported may be defined as:

$$T = a.[P^*_E Q^*_E]\qquad(4.8)$$

Where: a = the price of foreign exchange allocated to transport
     Q^*_E = quantity of food imported
     P^*_E = price of other essentials imported

In Kenya, quantities of food imported are exogenously determined by a decline in the per capita marketed surplus of food production available for urban consumption to formal marketing agencies. Therefore, as the international price of fuel or transport equipment rises, *ceteris paribus*, it becomes difficult for Kenyan farmers to buy importables because of the less availability of foreign exchange for importation of transport equipment.

For static analysis, we can assume that the total level of Kenyan exports are fixed so that:

$$(\partial M_T/\partial T) < 0 \qquad(4.9)$$

and also;

$$(\partial M_T/\partial T) > 0 \qquad(4.10)$$

This means that as internal marketing costs in the informal sector would increase both because of the direct effect of the increased fuel on domestic transport costs.

4.   THE ROLE OF DUALISTIC MARKETS

The official producer price of food crop may be defined as:

$$P_{Ff} = P_C - M_T - G_1 \qquad(4.11)$$

Where: G_1 = government revenue extracted from food crops

The informal market price becomes:

$$P_{Fi} < P_{CFi} < M_{ti} \qquad(4.12)$$

Where: P_{CFi} = consumer price of food in the informal market

M_{ti} = transaction costs in the informal market

When the price of importables increases, the producer price of food in the informal market becomes:

$$(P_{Fi}) > (P_{Ff}) \tag{4.13}$$

The producer price of the export crop may be defined as:

$$P_E = eP^*_E - M_T - G_2 \tag{4.14}$$

Where: G_2 = government revenue extracted from export crops
e = the exchange rate

Equation [4.14] demonstrates that given the export price, how an increase in the price of importables would make it difficult for Kenyan farmers to get available unit profit on their export crop unless the government alters the rate of extraction or the exchange rate. The model also assumes that no domestic consumption of export crops and therefore no welfare effects of reduced (P_E) or domestic consumer food production is assumed in the country, and the effect of reduced (P_F) should be to increase food consumption.

The price of non agricultural products is determined by:

$$P_N = eP^*_N + M_T + G_3 = [eP^*_N + M(aP) + G_3] \tag{4.15}$$

Where M_T = tax imposed on nonagricultural products and thus we assume that in the above equation marketing costs add on to the international price farmers pay.

5.   MATHEMATICAL DERIVATION OF AN ALTERNATIVE MODEL

The nominal rural household income is defined as:

$$Y_R = P_{Ff}Q_{Ff} + P_E Q_E + S_B + S_S + R \tag{4.16}$$

Where: P_E = producer prices of agricultural commodities exported
Q_E = quantities of agricultural commodities exported
S_B = subsidies received by the agricultural sector
S_S = social services provided by the rural sector
R = remittances of rural workers working in the non

agricultural sector

The quantity of export crops is expressed as a function of the following variables:
$$Q_E = Q_E(l, L, P_{Ff}, P_E, t_E, GR, ESE) \qquad (4.17)$$

Where: $t_E = t_E (GR)$
L = land
l = labor
ESE = expenditure on essentials imported
t_E = level of technology in the export crop sector
GR = government expenditure on agricultural investments

The nominal rural household income (Y_R) is defined as:

$$Y_R = P_{Ff}Q_{Ff} + P_EQ_E + S_S + S_B + R$$

As the income of households increases the poverty decreases. That is:
$$\text{Poverty} = aY_R, a < o$$
$$\text{Maximize } Y_R = P_{Ff}Q_{Ff} + P_EQ_E + S_S + S_B + R$$
$$\text{Subject to: } \{P_E, l, L, t_E, GR, P_{Ff}, ESE\}$$

As a result, the minimization of poverty is equivalent to the maximization of the rural nominal income. Thus our problem consists of determining the rural nominal income of households which will be maximized. The maximization of the income yields:

$$dY_R = 0$$
$$0 = dY_R = Q_{Ff}dP_{Ff} + P_{Ff}dQ_{Ff} + Q_EdP_E + P_EdQ_E + dS_B + dS_S + ESE \qquad (4.18)$$

From equation (4.17), we have:

$$\partial Q_E = \frac{\partial Q_E \partial l}{\partial l} + \frac{[\partial Q_E \partial L]}{\partial L} + \frac{[\partial Q_E \partial P_{Ff}]}{\partial P_{Ff}} + \frac{[\partial Q_E \partial P_E]}{\partial P_E} + \frac{\partial P_E}{\partial t_E} \cdot \frac{\partial t_E}{\partial GR} \partial GR + \frac{\partial Q_E}{\partial ESE} \partial ESE$$
$$(4.19)$$

Substituting equation (4.18) into equation (4.19), we obtain:

$$0 = Q_E \frac{\partial P_E}{P_E} + P_E \left[\frac{\partial Q_E}{\partial a} \partial a + \frac{\partial Q_E}{\partial L} \partial L + \frac{\partial Q_E}{\partial P_{Ff}} \partial P_{Ff} + \frac{\partial Q_E}{\partial ESE} \partial ESE - \frac{\partial Q_E}{\partial P_E} \partial P_E + \frac{\partial Q_E}{\partial T_E} \cdot \frac{\partial T_E}{\partial GR} \partial GR - \frac{\partial Q_E}{\partial GR} \frac{\partial Q_E}{P_N} \right]$$

$$+ \partial S_B + \partial S_S + \partial R$$

(4.20)

Re—arranging equation (4.20), we obtain:

$$Q_E = Q_{Ff} \frac{\partial P_{Ff}}{\partial P_E} - P_{Ff} \frac{\partial Q_{Ff}}{\partial P_E} - P_E \frac{\partial Q_E}{\partial a} \cdot \frac{\partial a}{\partial P_E} - P_E \frac{\partial Q_E}{\partial L} \cdot \frac{\partial L}{\partial P_E} - P_E \frac{\partial Q_E}{\partial ESE} ESE P_E \frac{Q_E}{P_E} - P_E \frac{\partial Q_E}{\partial E} \cdot \frac{\partial_E}{\partial GR} \frac{\partial GR}{P_E} -$$

$$P_E \frac{\partial Q_E}{\partial GR} \cdot \frac{\partial GR}{\partial P_E} \frac{\partial S_B}{P_E} \frac{\partial S_S}{\partial P_E} \frac{\partial R}{\partial P_E}$$

(4.21)

Assuming that **S$_B$**, **S$_S$** and **R** are roughly constant in agricultural third world and factoring out **dGR/dPE**, we obtain:

$$Q_E = Q_{Ff} \left(\frac{dP_{Ff}}{dP_E} \right) - P_E \left[\left(\frac{\partial Q_E}{\partial a} \right) \left(\frac{dL}{dP_E} \right) \right] - P_E \left[\left(\frac{\partial Q_E}{\partial L} \right) \left(\frac{dL}{dP_E} \right) \right] - P_E \left[\left(\frac{\partial Q_E}{\partial P_{Ff}} \right) \left(\frac{dP_{Ff}}{dP_E} \right) \right]$$

$$- P_E \left(\frac{\partial Q_E}{\partial P_E} \right) - P_E \left[\left(\frac{\partial Q_E}{\partial T_E} \right) \left(\frac{\partial T_E}{\partial GR} \right) \left(\frac{\partial Q_E}{\partial GR} \right) \right] \frac{dGR}{dP_E} - P_E \left[\left(\frac{\partial Q_E}{\partial ESE} \right) dESE \right]$$

(4.22)

Also we have:

$$\frac{dl}{dP_E} = \left\{ \frac{dl}{dP_E} \bullet \frac{P_E}{I} \right\} \bullet \frac{I}{P_E} = e_{l, PE} \left(\frac{I}{P_E} \right)$$ (4.23)

Where **e$_{lPE}$** is the elasticity of labor with respect to the price of exported crops.

$$\frac{dL}{dP_E} = \left\{ \left(\frac{dL}{dP_E} \right) \left(\frac{P_E}{L} \right) \right\} \frac{L}{P_E} = e_{L, P_E} \left(\frac{L}{P_E} \right)$$ (4.24)

Where e_L, P_E is the elasticity of the cultivated area with respect to the price of the exported crops.

$$\frac{dP_{Ff}}{dP_E} = \left\{ \left(\frac{dP_{Ff}}{dP_E} \right) \left(\frac{P_E}{P_{Ff}} \right) \right\} \frac{P_{Ff}}{P_E} = e_{PFf} P_E P_{Ff} P_E \quad (4.25)$$

Where $e_{PFf} P_E$ is the elasticity of the food price in the formal sector with respect to that of the exported crop

$$\frac{dQ_E}{dP_E} = \left\{ \left(\frac{dQ_E}{dP_E} \right) \left(\frac{P_E}{Q_E} \right) \right\} \frac{Q_E}{P_E} = eP_E \left(\frac{Q_E}{P_E} \right) \quad (4.26)$$

Where eP_E is the price elasticity of exported crop

$$\frac{dGR}{dP_E} = \left\{ \left(\frac{dGR}{dP_E} \right) \left(\frac{P_E}{GR} \right) \right\} \frac{GR}{P_E} = e_{GR}, P_E \left(\frac{GR}{P_E} \right) \quad (4.27)$$

Where $e_{GR} P_E$ is the elasticity of government expenditure with respect to the price of exported crop

$$\frac{dESE}{dP_E} = \left(\frac{dESE}{dP_E} \right) \left(\frac{P_E}{ESE} \right) \frac{ESE}{P_E} e_{ESE}, _{PE} \left(\frac{ESE}{P_E} \right) \quad (4.28)$$

Where $e_{ESE,PE}$ is the elasticity of expenditure on other essential importable with respect to the price of exported crops.

Replacing $\dfrac{dl}{dP_E}$, $\dfrac{dL}{dP_E}$, $\dfrac{dP_{Ff}}{dP_E}$, $\dfrac{dQ_E}{dP_E}$, $\dfrac{dGR}{dP_E}$ and $\dfrac{dESE}{dP_E}$ by their respective

expressions in terms of their elasticities in equation (4.28), we obtain:

$$Q_E = \left[\left(\frac{1}{1} + e_{PE} \right) \left(\frac{dP_{Ff}}{dP_E} \right) \right] Q_{Ff} - \left[\left(\frac{1}{1} + e_{PE} \right) \left(\frac{dQ_{Ef}}{dP_E} \right) \right] P_{Ff} - \left[\frac{1}{1} + e_{PE} \left(\frac{dQ}{dl} \right) e_{IPE} \right] - \left[\left(\frac{1}{1} + e_{Fe} \right) \left(\frac{dQ}{dL} \right) e_{LE} \right] L$$

$$- \left\{ \left(\frac{1}{1} + e_{PE} \right) e_{GR} \left[\left(\frac{\partial Q_E}{\partial T_E} \right) \left(\frac{\partial T_E}{\partial GR} \right) + \left(\frac{\partial Q_E}{\partial GR} \right) \right] \right\} GR - \left[\frac{1}{1} + e_{PE} \left(\frac{dQ}{dESE} \right) e_{ESEPE} \right] ESE$$

$$(4.29)$$

We assume that:

$$\sim e_{PE} \sim < 1$$

Because agricultural third world countries have limited capacity of production. As a result,

$$1 + e_{PE} > 0 . \qquad (4.24)$$

Therefore, the signs of the coefficients in our equation (4.23) remain the same as those of equation (4.22).

HYPOTHESIS

The coefficient of the food price is expected to be positive. An increase in the price of food means that its quantity sold in this sector decreases. This decrease in the quantity of food also leads to the increase in the price of exported crops.

Thus, we expect:

$$-\frac{dP_{Ff}}{dP_E} < 0, \qquad -\frac{dQ_{Ff}}{dP_E} > 0 . \qquad (4.25)$$

Also an increase in the food price in the formal sector means that its quantity of exported crop decreases.

We expect the coefficient of the quantity of labor used in export production:

$$-\frac{1}{1 + eP_E} \bullet \frac{\partial Q_E}{\partial} \bullet elP_E > 0 . \qquad (4.26)$$

An increase in the quantity of labor increases the output **(QE)** and decreases the price. As a result:

$$e \ lPE = (\partial l / \partial PE) . (PE/l) < 0, \text{and } \partial \ QE / \partial l > 0. \quad (4.27)$$

It follows that:

$$[-1/(1 + ePE) . (\partial QE / \partial l) . (elPE)] > 0$$

Similarly, we expect the coefficient of labor to be positive.

We expect the coefficient of food price in the formal sector to be positive. The increase in the price of food in the formal sector leads to the decrease in its quantity sold. This decrease in the quantity of food sold in the formal sector increases the price of exported crop.

Thus,
$$\frac{dQ_{Ff}}{dP_E} < 0. \tag{4.28}$$

As a result,
$$\frac{-dQ_{Ff}}{dP_E} > 0.$$

Finally,
$$-\left[\left(\frac{1}{1+eP_E}\right)\left(\frac{dQ_{Ff}}{dP_E}\right)eP_{Ff}P_E\right] > 0. \tag{4.29}$$

That is the coefficient of food price in the formal sector is expected to be positive.

We expect the coefficient of government expenditure:

$$\left[-\frac{1}{1}+1+e_{PE}\left(\left(\frac{\partial Q_E}{\partial T_E}\right)\left(\frac{\partial T_E}{\partial GR}\right)+\left(\frac{\partial Q_E}{\partial GR}\right)\right)e_{GRPE}\right] > 0 \tag{4.30}$$

An increase in government expenditure leads to the improvement of technology in export sector:

$$\frac{\partial T_E}{\partial GR} > 0 \tag{4.31}$$

which in turn increases the quantity of exported crop:

$$\frac{\partial Q_E}{\partial T_E} > 0. \tag{4.32}$$

This results in the decrease in the price of exported crop. That is:

$$eGRP_E = \left(\frac{\partial GR}{\partial P_E}\right)\left(\frac{P_E}{GR}\right) < 0 \text{ and } \frac{\partial Q_E}{\partial GR} > 0 \tag{4.33}$$

Thus: $$\left[\left(\frac{\partial Q_E}{\partial T_E}\right)\left(\frac{\partial T_E}{\partial GR}\right)+\left(\frac{\partial Q_E}{\partial GR}\right)\right]eGRP_E < 0 \qquad (4.34)$$

It follows that:

$$-[(1/1+eGRPE)(\partial\ QE/\partial\ tE).(\ \partial tE/GR)+(\partial\ QE/GR)).eGRPE] > 0 \quad (4.35)$$

Finally, we expect the coefficient of the expenditure on essential importables to be positive.

$$\left(\frac{-1}{1+e_{PE}}\right)\left(\frac{\partial Q_E}{\partial ESE}\right)e_{ESE,PE} \qquad (4.36)$$

An increase in the expenditure on essential imports increases the quantity of exported crop and decreases its price. As a result:

$$\frac{\partial Q_E}{\partial ESE} > 0 \qquad (4.37)$$

And: $$e_{ESE,PE} = \left(\frac{\partial ESE}{\partial P_E}\right)\left(\frac{P_E}{ESE}\right) < 0 \qquad (4.38)$$

Thus: $$\left(\frac{\partial Q_E}{\partial ESE}\right)e_{ESE,PE} < 0 \qquad (4.39)$$

It follows that: $$\left(\frac{-1}{1+e_{PE}}\right)\left(\frac{\partial Q_E}{\partial ESE}\right)e_{ESE,PE} > 0 \qquad (4.41)$$

This means that we expect the coefficient of the expenditure on essential imports to be positive.

The final equation of the alternative model we will estimate will be:

$$QE = a_0 + a_1 Q_{Ff} + a_2 P_{Ff} + a_3 I + a_4 L + a_5 GR + a_6 ESE \qquad (4.42)$$

a_0 is a constant
$a_1>0;\ a_2<0;\ a_3>0;\ a_4<0;\ a_5>0;\ a_6>0.$

Policy Implications

The regression results of the first model are given below:
$$\text{poverty} = 18.834 - 0.0007GR - 0.0176Y + 0.004APF$$
$$\phantom{\text{poverty} = 18.834} (-4.223) \quad (-4.838) \quad (1.906)$$
Adjusted R—squared = 98.5
DW = 3

The above results were derived from running the regression whereby poverty is a dependent variable. The coefficient of government revenue is negative indicating an inverse relationship between increase in government expenditure on agricultural investments and a reduction in poverty. The t—statistic is highly significant at 5 percent level. This confirms our hypothesis that there exists an inverse relationship between government expenditure on agricultural investment and poverty alleviation.

The coefficient of rural income is negative indicating that there is an inverse relationship between increase in rural household income and reduction in poverty. The t—statistic is significant at ten percent level. This highlights the significance of the increase in rural household income in the reduction of poverty.

The coefficient of actual price of food is negative indicating that increase in the price of food will lead to the reduction in poverty. The beneficiaries of the increase in food prices goes directly to the revenue received by the rural household thus reducing poverty. The t—statistic of rural household income is significant indicating a major role that producer prices plays in poverty alleviation in this analysis.

The Durbin—Watson is 3.0 indicating there is no serial correlation in the model. The adjusted R—squared is 98.5, indicating that the government expenditure on agricultural sector, rural household income and producer price of food explain 98.5 percent of the level of poverty in Kenya. Since rural household income is highly significant and given that its increase decreases poverty, we maximize it in order to determine the key variables which reduce poverty in Kenya. Thus, we use an alternative model. The regression results of the mathematical model given in equation (41)

The regression results of the alternative mathematical model given in equation (41) are shown below followed by the policy implications of these results.

$$\text{Exports} = -1718.061 + .000191ESE - 0.4658APF + 0.16667AQF -$$
$$\phantom{\text{Exports} = -1718.061} (4.516) \quad (-1.550) \quad (5.830)$$
$$.01034LAND + 0.04995LABOR + 0.3413GR$$
$$ (-1.225) \quad (0.0803) \quad (2.2498)$$
Adjusted R—squared = 98.5
DW = 3.05

The coefficient of **ESE** expenditure on (essential imports) is positive, indicating that there is a positive relationship between exports and expenditure on essentials. This includes inputs such as fertilizers, spare parts and pesticides needed in the food sector. If the essentials imports decreases exports will also decrease. The t—statistic of **ESE** is significant at 5 percent level.

The coefficient of (**APF**), the actual price of food is negative (—4658) indicating an inverse relationship between exports and the actual price of food. Increase in actual price of food leads to a decrease in exports. This may be so because foreign buyers of Kenyan food can get a cheaper food in other countries. Additionally, Kenyan producers can directly sell their food on the domestic market since they can get substantial revenue from their domestic sale.

The t—statistic is significant at ten percent level of significance. The coefficient of actual quantities of food (**AQF**) is positive. This explains that there is an increase in actual quantities of food leads to an increase in export because there is enough food to export and consume locally.

The coefficient of land is negative indicating that there is a negative relationship between the cultivated land and the increase in export because the land exhibits diminishing returns. Moreover, the t—statistics is not significant, indicating that increase in cultivated land does not play a major role in the alleviation of poverty in Kenya.

The coefficient of labor is positive meaning that increase in labor in the export production sector leads to increase in exports. However, the t—statistic is not significant. The reason is because the export crops in Kenya are capital intensive[xiv].

The coefficient of government revenue used in agricultural sector technological improvement and infrastructure is positive. This tells us that when the government invests in agricultural research, education, roads, machinery and technology would lead to increase in exports. The t—statistic is highly significant at a 5 percent level, thus confirming the importance of government expenditure as a factor in increasing export volume.

The adjusted R—squared is 98.5 which means the fitness of the model is 98.5 percent in explaining the dependent variable. The Durbin—Watson is 3.05 indicating that there is no serial correlation in the model. It appears that the determinants of poverty or the key variables which can alleviate poverty by maximizing rural household income are government expenditure on agricultural sector, the quantity of food produced, expenditure on essential importables, and the price of food produced.

The above empirical results indicate that actual prices of food (**APF**) have an inverse relationship with exports meaning that increase in the price of food leads to decrease in exports. The coefficient is negative, indicating the inverse relationship which may suggest that increase in food price locally leads to the increase in its supply on the domestic market. Thus, reducing exports.

These policy implications should take into account the specific situation of women in agricultural production. It can be shown that in Africa women play a dominant role in agricultural production and yet income received from agriculture is not directed to women. Women in sub—Saharan Africa have a predominant role in agricultural production; a fact which has been substantiated by a number of researchers. One of the pioneering syntheses on this issue is contained in Ester Boserup's work. Boserup reviewed studies which had been made in African villages (most of which was carried out in 1950s and 1960s) and found out that, in general, more women than men in cultivator families were doing agricultural work, and women were usually working more hours per week in agriculture than men. As a result, in most all cases, women were found to do around 70 percent and in one case nearly 80 percent of the total work[xv]. It should be noted that Boserup was considering total agricultural production, including cash crops where men are more heavily involved.

Part of the explanation for the importance of women in providing sustenance for the family is the prevalence among Africans of a particular concept of the child—bearing role of women. Success at both child bearing and food production is essential to women. In view of society, and especially in the eyes of the women themselves, child bearing is basic to their reason for living, the very essence of their femaleness, raising food to feed the children is part of their nurturing role. To fail in this realm would be to fail as a mother and as a person. Under these conditions, food crop production can be seen as women's work' per excellence, and men would be understandably reluctant to take it over. As Theresa Thongko points out, a man performing a duty which is looked upon as that of female is ridiculed as is a woman who performs labor assigned to males[xvi].

It must also be emphasized that women take considerable pride in their agricultural work and derive personal satisfaction from their productivity. Unfortunately, most of those who have written about the women's agricultural activities have either emphasized the back—breaking nature of their toil and the observer's desire to get the women out of the hot sun and into their houses, or decried the fact that women have been left behind in the traditional sector while men have moved into modern occupations[xvii]. Both approaches ignore the wishes and attitudes of the women toward their work[xviii].

Analysis of this data confirms the fact that the cases presented by researchers such as Boserup represent a general phenomenon in sub—Sahara Africa. In addition, it indicates that the importance of female labor in agriculture in the region is quite different from overall importance of female labor in agriculture worldwide (summarized in the table below). The data on sub—Saharan Africa included in table 11 below is based on a random, independent sample of sub—Saharan societies. The distribution of labor found in that sample is compared to the distribution in word wide base and confirms the women exploitation in Africa.

TABLE 4.1   Division of Labor

Area	Male Predominance	Female Predominance	Equal Participation	Total
Sub— Saharan Africa	10 (19%)	27 (52%)	15 (29%)	52 (100%)
World	92 (47%)	67 (34%)	38 (19%)	197 (100%)

Source: Bryson Judy, Journal of Development Studies: April 1981 p.37

One of the major reasons that women have not obtained a fair share in agricultural revenue is because in large parts of Sub—Saharan Africa, women are solely responsible for the production and sale of certain food crops. They are often but not always entitled to the harvest from their production and are responsible for providing food for their children.

A number of studies have pointed out that the importance of female labor in production tends to be lower in Kenya because of capital intensity of the techniques of agricultural production (such as tractors, crop rotation or cultivation practices which entails fertilization to achieve higher yields per unit of land) than in extensive systems. The results shown in table 12 shows the predominance of female participation in agriculture.

TABLE 4.2   Division of Labor by Gender

Type of Cultivation System	Male Predominance	Female Predominance	Equal Participation	Total
Horticulture	17 (17%)	52 (50%)	35 (33%)	104 (100%)
Agriculture	75 (81%)	15 (16%)	3 (3%)	93 (100%)

Source: Bryson: Women and Agriculture in sub—Saharan Africa : Implications for Development (An Explanatory Note). Journal of Development Studies Vol.17 No. 3 April 1981.

Abundant empirical evidence also exists both in Africa to suggest that women's access to agricultural extension, production, credit, and inputs from the formal official agencies is considerably more constrained than men's, all leading to efficiency losses in production. In addition to improved rules and regulations, ensuring women's access to services may necessitate the employment of female extension and credit agents and organization of special training programs for women farmers, as well as women's more active participation in the organizations that control these resources. Also, to the extent that land is needed as collateral to obtain credit/or access of women producers to input, their lack of land ownership must adversely affect their access to these services.

The growing amount of literature on women's political economic issues that has appeared during the last ten years covered by this study has been instrumental in deepening our understanding of the nature and extent of women's participation in economic activities. It has also increased our awareness of the conceptual and empirical results that exists regarding women's policy concerns. One such problem is the definition and measurement of women's work. As studies on women's labor force participation have proliferated, the inadequacies of available statistics in capturing the degree of their participation in economic life has become progressively more obvious.

Many studies have excluded data on women participation in the labor force because these studies do not see their role as anything but just a role they play as part of their existence. Survey work, detailed studies of women's activities, and even mere observation of everyday life has led to a general agreement about the obscurity and low value generally attached to women's work in many societies and not confined to Kenya alone[xix]. There are in fact two issues that are inter—related along these lines. One is ideological and is associated with the tendency to regard to women's work as secondary and subordinate to men's. An aspect of this tendency relates to the fact that an important proportion of women's work is unpaid. Both the ideological and monetary aspects are clearly symbolized by an expression such as 'my mother doesn't work' even though she might be working longer hours than any other household member. 'Work' in this case means participation in paid production, income generating activity. The ideological aspect is reinforced by the pervasive lack of clear conceptualization of the role played by women at different levels of economic life.

The ideological bias is deeply embedded in most of the concepts widely used in social sciences; dealing with it requires an effort to analyze the very roots of this bias and to reconstruct these concepts in such a way that the role of women in society can be placed in its proper perspective[xx].

The second issue is a consequence of the statistical bias mentioned above and is of a less fundamental but more practical nature. It refers to the actual statistical evaluation and accounting of women's work either as participants in the labor force or in terms of GNP estimation. It is by now well known most labor force and accounting statistics reflect a gross under—estimation of women's role in activity. Concern over this problem has been growing during the past decade. Boserup, in her analysis of women's role in the development process, put it clearly when she wrote that 'the subsistence activities usually omitted in the statistics of production and incomes are largely women's work[xxi]. This concern has been expressed repeatedly by other authors as well[xxii]. Yet subsistence production is not the only area of underestimating of the women's work.

Although we do not want to fall into the trap of making a fetish of statistics, it is important to point out shortcomings of available data for the purposes of evaluating women's work. Those data are commonly used for planning purposes and can be the source of numerous biases. The purpose of this policy analysis is to show how the shortcomings described above have prevented women from attaining the fair share of the revenue although they contribute the major portion of the total revenue.

Given the unfair distribution of resources between men and women that we discussed above we therefore recommend policies that are based on equitable distribution of resources so that women can get their fair share of revenue obtained from agricultural produce.

The first major policy is to channel essential inputs to women and to allow women to have access to land rights that have been denied due to the ideological reasons we described earlier. This will allow women to exercise their rights whereby their can choose to grow export cash crops rather the subsistence crops which are for home consumption only.

The traditional positioning of women within the farming system should be eliminated so that women can choose to work anywhere within the farming system. This is always done by customarily assigning women to task based on gender rather than ability. This division of labor based on gender and crops created a very well established division of labor between men and women. This has led to differences between land types and crops and thus has created unequal distribution of income between men and women[xxiii].

A number of studies of have drawn attention to a sexual division of labor in third world agriculture, where men and women are either responsible for separate field operations or they cultivate crops. While recognizing this, few have gone to explore the corollary: that there may be a parallel division in the control of crops. As a result, most agricultural development projects have been based on an implicit assumption that, regardless of how labor is organized, all cultivation is carried out on behalf of the 'household unit', and that the land, labor, crops and finances are under the control of the 'household' head. The latter is usually the only direct participant in agricultural development projects, as planners assume that the other household members will automatically take part and that any increased income accruing to the head will also benefit them. Therefore, failure to involve women in development and farming systems has not only increased their economic dependence on men but is also a major reason for deficiencies in these activities and low national agricultural production.

To allow women to gain their fair share in the revenue resulting from production, government policy should pay a higher price for crops that are solely produced by women. This will increase their rural income.

This dissertation has shown empirically that the size of agricultural exports and prices are significant determinants of poverty in Kenya. The study concluded the following relationships on the determinants of poverty in Kenya:

    (i) The increase in the price of food increases poverty.

    (ii) The increase in government expenditure in agricultural sector decreases

       poverty.

    (iii) The increase in rural household income decrease poverty.

(iv) The increase in expenditure on essential importables increases exports of
   crops.

(v) The decrease in the price of crops increases their exports.

(vi) The increase in quantities of crops increases exports.

Given the above empirical results we can now suggest policy recommendations concerning poverty alleviation in Kenya. The study starts from the government expenditure on technology in agricultural sector. The government should increase its expenditure on technology in agricultural sector so that the export output will increase which in turn increases household income and thereby alleviates poverty.

It is noticeable that increase in imports of essentials will increase exports and in turn alleviate poverty. Therefore, the government should subsidize the importation of essentials by farmers so that they can save some of the cost of their production. This will lead to the increase of importables and the export output in the event that they spent more money on importables. This in turn will increase export and rural household income thus alleviating poverty.

Based on the empirical results it can be concluded that decrease in price of crops leads to increase of exports. Therefore it is recommended that the government should subsidize the actual price of food so that it would lead to increase in exports thus reducing poverty. This is so because when the price of exports is low its demand increases leading to an increase in rural household income which in turn reduces poverty. This is due to our earlier finding that there exits an inverse relationship between the increase in income and poverty reduction.

The increase in quantities of food increases the exports and thus reduces the poverty. Because of this then we can recommend that the government should increase its expenditure on technological training for new farming techniques. This is so because improvement in farming techniques will reduce cost of production and leads to increase in output due to efficiency associated with it.

V. THE IMPACT OF HIV/AIDS ON POVERTY IN AFRICA

Introduction

This section discusses the economic impact of HIV/AIDS. It begins by showing the global impact of the epidemic in respect to that of Africa. The study demonstrates that Aids has evolved from being an health issue to currently a developmental crisis. The demographic prevalence highlights the magnitude of the disease all over the countries of Africa. This is evidenced by its destruction of social capital especially the knowledge base of the society and the production sectors of agriculture and industry. The analysis shows how AIDS have weakened institutions leading to inhibition of economic growth thus creating wider and deeper poverty in the continent. It then traces the overall macroeconomic impact of the disease, followed by an in—depth analysis of its impact on households for both current and future generations, as well as other effects on the economy.

HIV/AIDS – The Medical Facts

1. What are HIV/AIDS?

AIDS (acquired immune deficiency syndrome) was first described only in 1981 and has become a major world-wide epidemic. AIDS is caused by infection with HIV (human immunodeficiency virus), which kills or harms cells of the body's immune system (T-cells), gradually destroying the body's ability to fight infections and certain cancers. There are two types of HIV: HIV-1, which is distributed world-wide; and HIV-2, which is largely confined to West Africa. Individuals diagnosed with AIDS are likely to get life-threatening diseases called opportunistic infections, which are caused by bacteria, viruses, and other types of microscopic organisms that are usually harmless in healthy people. AIDS is called "acquired" to distinguish it from inherited (genetic) forms of immunodeficiency. It is called a "syndrome" because it is a set of symptoms, which occur together, rather than a clear-cut disease.

2. The disease process

As HIV infection progresses, most people experience a gradual decrease in the number of cells in their blood called CD4+ T cells. These cells normally protect the body from infections and other types of disease.

Some people become so ill from the symptoms of AIDS that they are unable to hold a job or do household chores, while others may experience phases of intense life-threatening illness followed by periods of normal functioning. The term AIDS applies to the most advanced stages of HIV infection, and includes all HIV-infected people who have fewer than 200 CD4+ T cells, whereas healthy adults usually have counts of 1000 or more (The National Institute of Allergy and Infectious Diseases 2002).

Persistent or severe symptoms may not appear for a long time after HIV infection. However, HIV continues actively to infect and kill cells of the immune system, even when the person has no symptoms.

AIDS-defining opportunistic infections can be very severe, causing significant morbidity and death in people with HIV. However, use of highly active antiretroviral therapy and effective prophylactics and treatments for the infections can significantly mitigate the incidence of these complications.

Symptoms of opportunistic infections common in people with AIDS include:

- Coughing an shortness of breath

- Seisures and lack of co-ordination

- Difficult or painful swallowing

- Mental symptoms such as confusion and forgetfulness

- Severe and persistent diarrhea

- Fever

- Vision loss

- Nausea, abdominal cramps, and vomiting

- Wight loss and extreme fatigue

- Severe headaches

- Coma

For AIDS patients in Africa, tuberculosis (TB) is the most fatal of the opportunistic diseases.

3. How HIV spreads

HIV is relatively difficult to transmit, as it does not live for long outside the body. HIV spreads most often by sexual contact with an infected partner. The virus enters the body through the lining of the vagina, vulva, penis, rectum, or mouth during sex.

HIV also spreads through contact with infected blood. Before 1985, HIV was transmitted through transfusions of contaminated blood or blood components such as those given to people with haemophilia. Today, pre-donor screening and heat-treating techniques for blood products have practically eliminated the risk of getting HIV from transfusions.

HIV often spreads among users of intravenous (injected) drugs by sharing needles or syringes contaminated with blood from an infected individual. However, transmission by accidental needle insertions or other medical contact between patients and health care workers is rare (The National Institute of Allergy and Infectious Diseases 2002).

Women can transmit HIV to their babies during pregnancy or while giving birth. HIV can also spread to babies through the breast milk of infected mothers. Among 30 % of infected mothers transmit the disease to their babies.

Although HIV can be found in the saliva of infected individuals, no evidence exists that the virus can spread by contact with saliva, such as by kissing. In fact, saliva contains natural compounds that reduce the ability of HIV to cause infection. There is also no evidence that HIV is spread through sweat, tears or urine.

HIV is not spread through casual contact such as the sharing of food utensils, towels and bedding, swimming pools, telephones, or toilet seats. Nor is HIV spread by biting insects such as mosquitoes or bedbugs.

Having a sexually transmitted disease (STD) such as syphilis, genital herpes, chlamydial infection, gonorrhoea, or bacterial vaginosis appears to make people more susceptible to getting HIV infection during sex with infected partners.

4. How is HIV infection diagnosed?

Because early HIV infection often causes no symptoms, a doctor or other health care provider usually has to diagnose it by testing a person's blood for the presence of antibodies (disease-fighting proteins) to HIV. HIV antibodies generally do not reach detectable levels in the blood for one to three months following infection. It may take the antibodies as long as six months to be produced in quantities large enough to show up in standard blood tests. Babies born to mothers infected with HIV may or may not be infected with the virus, but all carry their mothers' antibodies to HIV for several months. If these babies lack symptoms, a doctor cannot make a definitive diagnosis of HIV infection using standard antibody tests until after 15 months of age (NIAID, 2002).

5. How is HIV infection treated?

Over the past 10 years, researchers have developed drugs to fight both HIV infection and its associated infections and cancers. These drugs may slow the spread of HIV in the body and delay the onset of opportunistic infections. Because HIV can become resistant to any of these drugs, health care providers must use a combination treatment to suppress the virus effectively. Currently available antiretroviral drugs do *not* cure people of HIV infection or AIDS, however, and they all have side effects that can be severe.

While highly active antiretroviral therapy (HAART) is not a cure for AIDS, it has greatly improved the health of many people with AIDS and it can reduce the amount of virus circulating in the blood to nearly undetectable levels. Research has shown that HAART cannot entirely eradicate HIV from the body.

6. How can HIV infection be prevented?

Because no preventive vaccine for HIV is available, the only way for individuals to prevent infection by the virus is to avoid behaviours that put a person at risk of infection, such as having unprotected sex and sharing needles. Behavioural interventions are likely to remain the backbone of HIV prevention for the foreseeable future (Adler, 2001).

However, governments and organisations can take action to reduce the numbers of the newly infected other than by trying to change people's risky behaviour.

First, diagnosis of infected individuals has an important role in secondary prevention, because it allows infected individuals to benefit from possible treatment to reduce the chance of progression to severe immunodeficiency. Identifying those who are HIV positive in order to work with them to prevent onward virus transmission is also fundamental to primary HIV prevention (Adler, 2001). Promotion of voluntary HIV testing and promotion of counselling are therefore an important strategy to prevent the spread of HIV.

Second, as stated in section 3, there is substantial evidence that STI's may increase the susceptibility of uninfected individuals to HIV and also increase the infectiousness of HIV-positive individuals. This is because of sore or injured
mucous membrane and because an infectious process is already occurring. Control of STIs therefore has an important role in the primary prevention of HIV. Screening of STIs and early treatment of syphilis, genital herpes, chlamydial infection, etc would therefore be effective in reducing the rate of newly infected individuals, and it offers an opportunity to focus behavioural interventions.

Third, testing blood samples for HIV antibody and excluding those at increased risk from HIV from donating blood will minimise the risk of HIV transmission through blood transfusion.

Fourth, antiretroviral drugs have proven to be effective in preventing transmission of HIV from an infected mother to her baby. Until recently zidovudine drugs (AZT and ZDV)[1] known to hinder mother to child transmission (MTCT) were preferred. The standard AZT regimen is, however, too expensive and impractical for widespread use in developing countries. A joint Uganda-U.S. study found in 1999 a highly effective and safe drug regimen for MTCT prevention that is more affordable and practical than any other[2]. Patients were treated either with AZT or with nevirapine. The results demonstrated that a single oral dose of the antiretroviral drug nevirapine[3] given to HIV-infected women in labour and another to their babies within three days of birth reduced the transmission rate by half compared with those given a similar short course of AZT. At 14 to 16 weeks of age, 13.1 percent of infants who received nevirapine were infected with HIV, compared with 25.1 percent of those in the AZT group (US Department for Health and Human Services, 1999). Without any treatment 30-35 % of the infants of HIV-infected mothers become infected.

Nevirapine, developed by Boehringer Ingelheim Pharmaceuticals (BIP), is a non-nucleoside reverse transcriptase inhibitor, and is in a different class of antiviral drugs than AZT. Nevirapine is rapidly absorbed and transferred across the placenta to the infant, and it breaks down slowly. It can

89

be easily stored at room temperature. The cost of the drug used in the nevirapine regimen is approximately 200 times cheaper than the long-course AZT, and almost 70 times cheaper than a short course of AZT given to the mother during the last month of pregnancy.

On 7 July 2000, BIP announced that it would offer the antiretroviral drug nevirapine (Viramune®) free of charge for use in prevention of mother to child transmission for a period of five years in developing countries. BI announced that it would make this donation in partnership with the United Nations family (UNAIDS, 2001c). UNAIDS and WHO have recommended the use of nevirapine in MTCT prevention since October 2000, and confirmed their recommendation in a press release in March 2002 (UNAIDS, 2002). It is estimated that 600 000 infants get infected each year as a result of MTCT. This number could be halved with a wide distribution of nevirapine to mothers and babies in developing countries. The mother can take a pill when the labour begins and the child should be brought to a hospital and be given a dose within 72 hours of birth.

7. An HIV/AIDS vaccine?

Developing countries urgently need an AIDS vaccine to improve the effectiveness of their AIDS prevention programs. However, global spending on AIDS vaccine R&D is pitifully small — only $300-600 million/year, and focused on the strains of the virus and the eventual market in North America and Western Europe. A number of institutions, including the World Bank and the European Commission, have been searching for new mechanisms and market incentives that would raise levels of private R&D and speed development of an AIDS vaccine that would be effective and affordable in developing countries.

There have been a number of different vaccine candidates. None of them has so far turned out to be effective. Currently a therapeutic vaccine is being tested clinically in Norway. It is being used on already infected people. The goal of the vaccine is to strengthen the body's own ability to fight the HIV virus and to hinder development of AIDS. The manufacturer hopes to get the vaccine ready for commercial release within three to five years (Juuko, 2002).

FIGURE 5.1

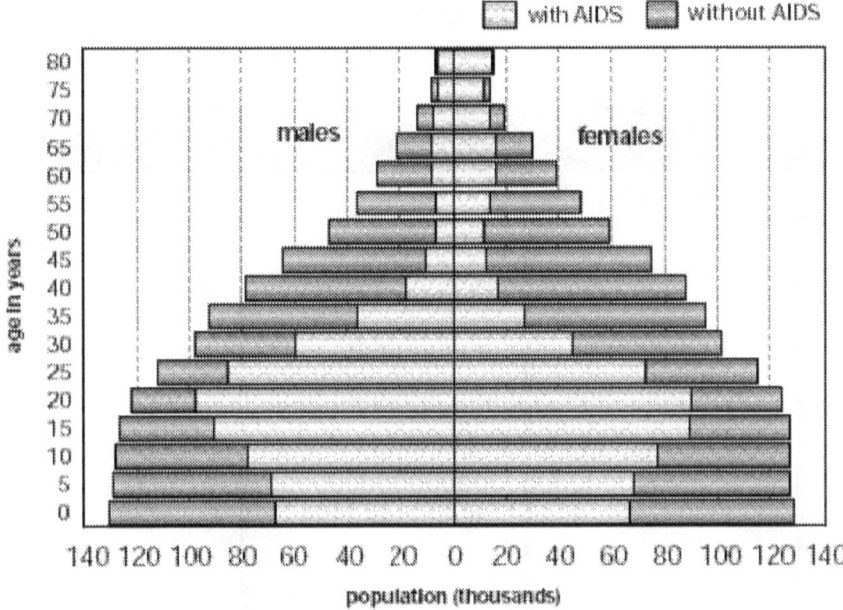

THE GLOBAL PROPORTIONAL IMPACT OF HIV/AIDS

Many social scientist and policy makers used to view Aids as an health issue to now becoming a developmental crisis. It is a tragic irony that almost three decades after the Alma—Ata Declaration elevated health to the status a basic and fundamental human right and explicitly recognized its relationship with economic development, we are witnessing, at the threshold of a new millennium, what may amount to the biggest health and development challenge the world has ever confronted— a disease which UNAIDS correctly notes, is unique in its devastating impact on the social, economic and demographic foundations of development. It is hard to believe that a disease, that was all but unknown barely two decades ago, has — to date — caused the death of 18.8 million people globally, among them 13.7 million from Africa alone. (UNAIDS 1999a).

The number of people infected with HIV in the world already reached an estimated thirty—four million with about 95 percent living in the developing world and a staggering 70 percent in Sub—Saharan Africa alone. What is more, the rate at which the epidemic is spreading is alarming. In 1999 alone, an estimated 5.4

million people were infected, a number which, when netted off against the estimated number of deaths (2.6 million), still increases the number of people infected
worldwide by 2.6 million (UNAIDS 1999a: 3)

TABLE 5.1   Global Summary of HIV/AIDS Epidemic (December 1999)

People newly infected with HIV in 1999	Total Adults Women Children < 15 years	5.4 million 4.7 million 2.3 million 620,000
Number of people living with HIV/AIDS	Total Adults Women Children < 15 years	34.3 million 33.0 million 15.7 million 1.3 million
AIDS deaths in 1999	Total Adults Women Children < 15 years	2.8 million 2.3 million 1.2 million 500,000
Total number of AIDS deaths since the beginning of the epidemic	Total Adults Women Children < 15 years	18.8 million 15.0 million 7.7 million 3.8 million
Total number of AIDS orphans since the beginning of the epidemic		13.2 million

Source: UNAIDS 2000. Global Summary of the HIV/AIDS Epidemic, end 1999.

The disease has taken on different forms in different parts of the world. In some
populations, the epidemics equally prevalent among men and women, in others,
certain vulnerable groups have been disproportionately affected (Anarfi et al.

1997; Orubuloye et al. 1993); in many cases the situation is dynamic and the disease has moved between different sub—populations evolving with time (Essex 1998: 427). Explanations for these distinct patterns are to be found in diverse factors including biology, behavior, gender, geography, culture, poverty, mobility and the interplay between (Mosesetal.1994J.Oppong 1998).

REGIONAL AND COUNTRY STATISTICS OF HIV/AIDS IN AFRICA

The African continent has the highest incidence of HIV/AIDS in the world today with some 23.3 million people infected. While the Global HIV/AIDS prevalence rate is 1.07%, the sub—Saharan African average is 8.57% (UNAIDS 2000:124). Across the continent, regional differences in HIV/AIDS prevalence are considerable, however no country has escaped the virus.

The countries with the highest prevalence rates are in the east, southern and central parts. The very worst affected countries on the Continent – indeed in the world – are in Southern Africa; Botswana has an infection rate of 35.80% and Zimbabwe 25.06% (UNAIDS 2000b; 2000c). In West Africa infection rates are climbing rapidly. Significant differences in rates of infection also exist within countries (J. Oppong 1998:437) among different sectors of the population, living in different parts of the country. National prevalence rates therefore, while capturing the overall infection rate of a country, often exhibit internal differences.

TABLE 5.2   The African HIV/AIDS Epidemic by country and region

Region / Country	Adult Rate (%)	Orphans Cumulative	Deaths 1999	Total Population
WESTERN AFRICA				
Benin	2.45	22,000	5,600	5,945,000
Burkina Faso	6.44	320,000	43,000	11,633,000
Cote d'Ivoire	10.76	420,000	72,000	14,534,000
Gambia	1.95	9,600	1,400	1,266,000
Ghana	3.60	17,000	33,000	19,699,000
Guinea	1.54	30,000	5,600	7,375,000
Guinea—Bissau	2.50	6,100	1,300	1,188,000
Liberia	2.80	31,000	4,500	2,941,000
Mali	2.03	45,000	9,900	10,976,000
Mauritania	0.52	——	610	2,602,000
Niger	1.35	31,000	6,500	10,414,000
Nigeria	5.06	1,400, 000	250,000	108,995,000
Reunion	——	——	——	690,000

Senegal	1.77	42,000	7,800	9,251,000
Sierra Leone	2.99	56,000	8,200	4,721,000
Togo	5.98	95,000	14,000	4,515,000
CENTRAL AFRICA				
Burundi	11.32	230,000	339,000	6,587,000
Cameroon	7.73	270,000	52,000	14,704,000
Central African Republic	13.84	99,000	23,000	3,550,000
Chad	2.69	68,000	10,000	7,462,000
Congo	6.43	53,000	8,600	2,867
Congo (DRC)	5.07	680,000	95,000	50,407,000
Equatorial Guinea	0.51	860	120	442,000
Gabon	4.16	8,600	2,000	1,196,000
Rwanda	11.21	270,000	40,000	7,238,000
EAST AFRICA				
Comoros	0.12	———	———	676,000
Eritrea	2.87	———	———	3,717,000
Ethiopia	10.63	1,200,000	280,000	61,123,000
Kenya	13.95	730,000	180,000	29,507
Madagascar	0.15	2,600	870	15,502,000
Mauritius	0.08	———	———	1,149,000
Somalia	———	———	———	9,718,000
Uganda	8.30	1,700,000	110,000	21,209,000
Tanzania	8.09	1,100,000	140,000	32,799,000
SOUTHERN AFRICA				
Angola	2.78	98,000	15,000	12,497
Botswana	35.80	66,000	24,000	1,592,000
Lesotho	23.57	35,000	16,000	2,108,000
Malawi	15.96	390,000	70,000	10,674,000
Mozambique	13.22	310,000	98,000	19,222,000
Namibia	19.54	67,000	18,000	1,689,000
South Africa	19.94	420,000	250,000	39,796,000
Swaziland	25.25	12,000	7,100	981,000

Zambia	19.95	650,000	99,000	8,974,000
Zimbabwe	25.06	900,000	160,000	11,509,000

Source: UNAIDS, 2000

Differences in the underlying biology of the virus partially explain geographic disparities in prevalence both globally and within Africa. 'The recognized differences in transmission and virulence of HIV—2, compared with HIV—1, indicate that HIV viruses can have different pathogenic potentials' (Kanki et al. 1999: 68). HIV—2 sub—types 'are less virulent and less transmissible in humans' (Essex 1998:427). In Africa – home to the worst of the epidemic – all ten HIV—1 sub-types have been reported and it has been established that within one population 'HIV—1 subtypes may themselves differ 'in their progression time to AIDS' (Kanki et al. 1999:68). HIV –1B, the strain of the virus that caused the epidemic in North America and Europe is all but absent in sub—Saharan Africa (Essex 1998:427).

FIGURE 5.2   Economic Growth Impact of HIV

Economic Growth Impact of HIV (1990-97)

Figure 2: Growth Impact of HIV (1990-97) (80 developing countries)

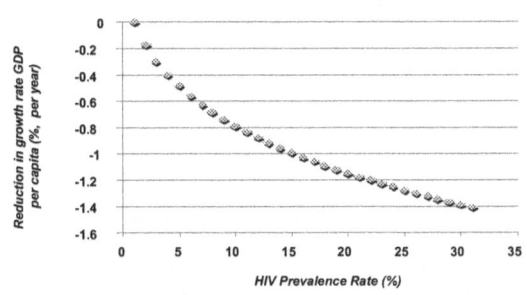

Source: R. Bonnel (2000) Economic Analysis ofHIV/AIDS, ADF2000 Background paper, World Bank

Health in general can affect economic performance through its impact on demography. Shorter life expectancy from HIV/AIDS prevalence will tend to inhibit investments in education and human capital accumulation, and where a greater proportion of the population becomes dependent, that is, consumes more resources than it produces, the rates of savings and capital investment and therefore of economic growth will be affected. (Kelly and Schmidt, 1996) HIV/AIDS has a devastating impact on the demographic profile of infected nations and reduces the size of the economically active population 'Projections from the US Census Bureau indicate that by 2003 Botswana, South Africa and Zimbabwe will be experiencing negative population growth' and that several other countries — including 'Malawi, Swaziland, Namibia and Zambia will see their population remain constant' a situation which until recently was believed to be improbable (Bonnel 2000, Annex 5: 2).While demographic projections vary in predicting the effects of the epidemic on population growth, there is general agreement that there will be a decrease in annual population growth in the region by 2010 (World Bank 1999: 13) In some countries, life expectancy has plummeted and is continuing to do so (Logie 1999). Between 1990 and 1995, out of eighteen Sub—Saharan counties which experienced 'declining' or 'stagnating' life expectancy rates, all but one (Togo) were undergoing a 'generalized' HIV/AIDS epidemic (World Bank 1999). In Botswana — Africa's most economically successful nation in recent years — 'a regional leader in literacy and healthcare' — life expectancy at birth will be cut *in half* over the next ten to twelve years, from perhaps sixty—five years down to about thirty—three, entirely as a result of HIV/AIDS (Essex 1999: 1). Hard won gains in development (achieved in recent decades) are fast unraveling.

FIGURE 5.3   Orphans Resulting from AIDS in Zambia

Orphans as a result of AIDS, Zambia

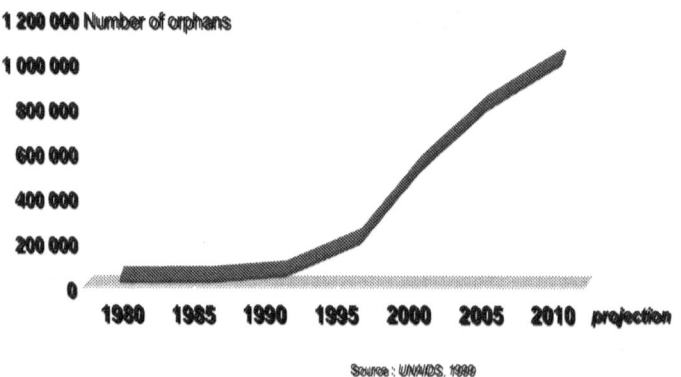

Source : UNAIDS, 1999

As already been shown, HIV/AIDS affects the most productive members of societies, therefore increasing the dependency ratio. More young children and older people – those less economically productive and more in need of care – are being supported by decreasing proportions of economically active adults (Cohen 1992: 2; Bollinger et al. 1999).

Not only is adult mortality increasing — as a result of the epidemic — but infant and child mortality has increased as well. Countries with high adult HIV/AIDS prevalence rates – such as Zambia and Kenya have also experienced a 'steep rise in child mortality' primarily due to vertical transmission (UNAIDS 1999: 22; Wekesa 2000). In fact 'a child born in Zambia or Zimbabwe today is more likely than not to die of AIDS' (World Bank 1999: 5). To date the epidemic has left 13.2 million orphans globally – currently 95% of the world's AIDS orphans live in Africa. In the worst affected countries, such as Zimbabwe, AIDS has orphaned 7% of *all* children under the age of fifteen (UNAIDS 2000: 27).

Significantly more women than men are living with HIV infection in sub— Saharan Africa (UNAIDS 1999a: 15). Social, economic and cultural factors as well as biological and economic conditions mean that women are disproportionately affected. The interplay of these factors and the nature and extent of gender inequality clearly differ contextually (C. Oppong 1995; Hamblin & Reid 1991). A key consideration is the difference in age patterns of HIV infection for men and women. Women tend to become infected younger for both biological and cultural reasons and for every ten African men infected, between twelve and thirteen women are infected (UNAIDS 1999a). In most African societies more men have extramarital partners than women (Caldwell 1993: 818; C. Oppong 1995: 42) and women are generally less informed about the potentially negative consequences of unprotected sex and/or are often unable to negotiate their sexual relations (UNAIDS 1999b).

Women may be forced into transactional sex through economic necessity and a real or perceived lack of market employment opportunities (UNAIDS 1999b). For example, in Ghana, in the early 1980's, the difficult economic situation created a substantial exodus of economic refugees who migrated temporarily into high HIV/AIDS prevalence regions and indulged in high—risk activities (J. Oppong 1998: 447; Anarfi et al 1997). Many of those who left the country were women. At the start of the epidemic in Ghana in 1996, *all* reported cases of HIV were female with a history of travel outside the country.

Migration then is undoubtedly an important factor in the spread of HIV/AIDS. Labor migration – with its resulting concentration of individuals in urban areas, the 'relaxation of social norms' and the adoption of risky behaviors — is associated with an increased risk of HIV/AIDS infection (Cohen 1992: 2; Seghal 1999: 5). Apart from the Ghanaian example there are countless others, such as the mines and commercial farms of Southern Africa with their concentrations of single men and widely available commercial and casual sex.

Changes in the numbers and composition of populations — as a result of HIV/AIDS — undoubtedly affect the ways in which societies are organized as well as the ways in which priorities are set for coping with the crisis. Nonetheless, 'while it is inevitable that massive rises in death among young, economically active adults will effect national economies, it is not easy to isolate or measure that effect' (UNAIDS 1999a: 17; Bollinger et al. 1999:7). The relationship between the epidemic and economic performance is a complex one, best illustrated by studying specific economic sectors and groups within populations.

The tremendous economic burden of HIV/AIDS and associated diseases is thus not limited to the current generation alone. "In essence, a high disease burden in a poor society can create a poverty trap, in which both disease and impoverishmemt are reproduced from one generation to the next" (Sachs, 2000).

World Bank's Studies have concluded that AIDS impact on Africa is devastating because it affects the most productive group of the population and this will lead to shortages in labor supply and costs associated with the deaths.

The economic effects of AIDS is imposed first to individuals and their families, then it moves to firms and businesses and the macro—economy. This paper will consider each of these levels and provide examples from various African countries to illustrate these impacts.

THE IMPACT OF HIV/ AIDS ON DEVELOPMENT IN AFRICA

1.   Economic Impact on Households

The household impact starts as soon as a member of the household begin to suffer from HIV—related illnesses:

i)   Loss of income of the patient who is frequently the main bread-winner

ii)   Reduced productivity

iii)   Household expenditures for medical expenses may increase substantially

iv)   Other members of the household, usually daughters and wives, may miss school or work less in order to care for the sick person

v)   Death results in: a permanent loss of income, from less labor on the farm or from lower remittances; funeral and mourning costs; and the removal of children from school in order to save on educational expenses and increase household labor, resulting in a severe loss of future earning potential.

vi)   Reduced consumption and investment due to dissaving

vii)   Increased counseling costs and rehabilitation

Studies in Tanzania, Cote d'Ivoire, Uganda, and Ethiopia have documented the tremendous burden of loss of income, large health care expenditures, reduced productivity, reallocation of resources and consumption of savings to pay for funeral expenditure (Stover, 1999)

- A case study of **Tanzania**, found that adult mortality was 8 percent of total household expenditure went to medical care and funerals in households that had an adult death in the preceding twelve months. In households with no adult death the figure was only 0.8 percent. In addition to increased expenditures, many households experienced a reduction in remittances if the adult member worked outside the home. In partial compensation for these financial setbacks, many households were forced to remove children from school in order to reduce education—related expenditures and have the children help with household chores.[24]

The cost of treatment and lost productivity

It is inadvisable to draw quick general patterns about the socio—impact of the disease in every location. However, there can be no doubt that the most immediate impacts of HIV/AIDS are felt at the individual and household level (Seghal 1999; Over, 1998;Bolinger et al, 1998)

Perhaps the most direct cost to households of HIV/AIDS and the one that is usually measured by cost of illness studies is the cost of treatment and the cost of work time that is lost. There is a wealth of literature on the subject which predictably cite costs including increased expenditures lost income and reallocation of responsibilities within the household Death brings further expenditures and the death of a mother often increases the probability of the death of her children. On the direct costs themselves, some studies estimate for instance that the cost of treatment and foregone productivity in Tanzania from a single HIV infection is about $2462—$5316 in 1985 dollars. High as these costs obviously are, the reality is that there are substantial additional secondary costs. (Sachs, 2000). When note is taken of the fact that most of the countries where the burden of the disease is particularly high are at the same time those with low incomes and a record of slow growth, it becomes clear that the most devastating impact of HIV/AIDS on an afflicted household is to dive it into poverty. The aids affliction itself becomes the cause of household poverty or the further exacerbation of poverty as households are driven into crippling levels of indebtedness and assets are depleted to pay for health care and other basic needs. According to the World Bank, a study of households and people that have become poorer over time showed that illness injury or death was the single most important cause.

An assessment of costs to the family will not be complete without mention of how the disease impacts on the most vulnerable groups within the household, namely widows and orphans.

Widows

An analysis of the impacts of the epidemic on young widows, in three districts in Uganda, found that the epidemic contributes to: an increase in female headed households; the feminization of poverty; 'crippling anxiety' over their sero—status and the infection of extended family members by the inherited widow (Topouzis et al. 1994). The profiles and case studies of individual women, clearly highlight the cumulative impacts of the disease and the vicious cycle of poverty that unfolds after the death of a husband in rural Africa.

Orphans

The impact of the disease on individual children depends on a variety of factors, such as their sex and age, the socio—economic status of their families, the number and age of their siblings etc. (Topouzis et al. 1994, Section 2:12). The care of these children often falls on the extended family – over—stretching their limited and declining resources. In many other scenarios, such as the one described by Ayieko in parts of Kenya, children have no caregivers in their households and 'manage their own household activities without the supervision of an adult' (Ayieko 1997: 11). Many children are therefore heading households and are: more likely to be out—of—school, malnourished, less likely to receive heath care, and are usually extremely poor. Many end up on the streets where they may be abused and sexually exploited, vulnerable to contracting HIV/AIDS (Ayieko 1997; World Bank 1999:14; UNAIDS 2000:26).

A study of children in three Ugandan districts found that orphaned children generally face the following situations, they may: be uprooted from towns and sent back to the village; run away from home to escape the stigma and poverty; taken out of school and sent to work; or sent to live with relatives or neighbors (Topouzis et al 1994). The impacts of the epidemic on the young people of Africa are clearly devastating. Opportunities for education and prospects of future income are being constrained and poverty – at individual, household and national levels — is on the increase (Bonnel 2000:15).

FIGURE 5.4   Funeral and Health Care Expenditures

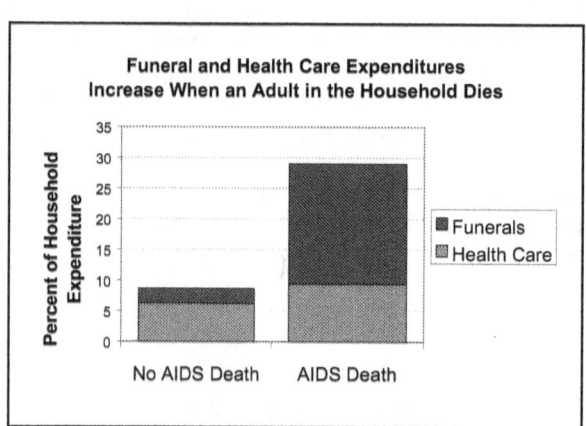

Source: Stover and Bollinger, 1999

- In **Cote d'Ivoire**, households with an HIV/AIDS patient spent twice as much on medical expenses as other households. Furthermore, 80 percent of the expenditures went to the AIDS patient, rather than to other household members who are ill. When the person with AIDS died or moved away, average consumption fell by as much as 44 percent during the following year.[25]

FIGURE 5.5   Household Impact of HIV/ AIDS

Impact of HIV/AIDS in urban households, Côte d'Ivoire

Source: *Simulation-based on data from Bechu, Delcroix and Guillaume, 1997*

- In **Uganda**, the economic impact of HIV—related deaths was stronger than other types of death, as households lost much of their savings in order to pay health care and funeral expenditures. Asset ownership declined when the death of an HIV+ member occured, but remained stable when the death was of an HIV— member.[26]
- In **Ethiopia**, a study of tweanty—five AIDS—afflicted rural families found that the average cost of treatment, funeral and mourning expenses amounted to several times the average household income.[27]

2.   Economic Impact on Agriculture

Agriculture is the largest sector in most African economies accounting for a large portion of production and a majority of employment. Studies done in Tanzania and other countries have shown that AIDS will have adverse effects on agriculture, including loss of labor supply and remittance income. The loss of a few workers at the crucial periods of planting and harvesting can significantly reduce the size of the harvest. In countries where food security has been a continuous issue because of drought, any declines in household production can have serious consequences. Additionally, a loss of agricultural labor is likely to cause farmers to switch to less—labor—intensive crops. In many cases this may mean switching from export crops to food crops.[28] Thus, AIDS could affect the production of cash crops as well as food crops.

Agriculture is the largest sector in most African economies, accounting for a large portion of production and employing the majority of workers' and earnings from agricultural exports pay for essential raw materials and imports necessary for

101

development (World Bank 1999: 16; Whiteside et al.2000: 3). Recognition of the impact of the HIV/AIDS epidemic on African agricultural is growing as is the fact that the costs of the epidemic are 'largely borne by rural communities' (Topouzis 1998: 7). The epidemic affects farm households by depleting both the 'human capital base' — 'through reducing the availability of labor skills and time, and the capital available through remittances or savings, which may disappear of be diverted to cover costs related to sickness and death' (Guerny 2000; UNAIDS 2000; Bollinger et al. 1999; Egal et al. 1999). The resulting impacts invariably affect both agricultural production and food security.

AIDS impacts agricultural production by reducing the area of land under cultivation. If less farm labor is available then more remote fields may be left to fallow and those under cultivation may receive less timely attention for tillage, planting and weeding, resulting in declining yields (UNAIDS 2000; Guerny 2000; Topouzis 1998; Over 1998). Crop varieties are declining and changes in cropping patterns are occurring. Cash crops are abandoned in favor of less labor—intensive subsistence crops (Guerny 2000; UNAIDS 2000; Topouzis 1998). Livestock production is also affected as animals are sold to generate cash or are sacrificed. Surviving households bear the added weight of feeding surviving children and women in particular are faced with the greatest burdens.

Thus the quality and quantity of food is rapidly declining in the hardest hit countries resulting in malnutrition and a reduction in food security. At the macro—economic level changes in the supply and quality of farm labor as well as changes in the supply and demand for agricultural produce, entailed by the epidemic, will alter the relative prices of commodities on local and international markets as well as interest rates and wages (Cohen 1992: 10).

• A study done by the **Zimbabwe** Farmers Union (ZFU) showed that the death of a breadwinner due to AIDS will cut the marketed output of maize in small scale farming and communal areas by 61 percent. Similar results were obtained for other crops (see table at right). The fall in marketed output results from losses of labor and remittances and the need to spend scarce resources on medical expenses.[29]

TABLE 5.3   **Market Output Reduction Due to AIDS in Zimbabwe**

Reduction in Marketed Output Due to AIDS Deaths in Zimbabwe	
Crops	Reduction in Marketed Output
Maize	61%
Cotton	47%
Vegetables	49%
Groundnuts	37%
Cattle Owned	29%

Source: P. Kwaramba 1997

- In **Ethiopia**, the male head of the household is responsible for special tasks, such as oxen cultivation, harvesting, threshing and farm management. One study found that the effect of an AIDS death varied by region: it would have the most severe effect on harvesting teff in Nazareth, on digging holes for transplanting enset plants in Atat, on ploughing millet fields in Baherdar, and on picking coffee in Yirgalem. Women are generally responsible for other tasks: leveling, weeding, harvesting minor crops, transporting produce, and household duties. The death of the wife to AIDS can make it difficult for other household members to carry out these tasks, in addition to caring for children. The death of a family member because of AIDS also leads to a reduction in savings and investment. The stock of food grain can be depleted to provide food for mourners and the other expenses were met most often by selling livestock. Such loss of productive assets only makes it harder to survive in the future.[30]

- In **Malawi**, 10 percent of GDP comes from estate agriculture. A recent study evaluated the costs of HIV/AIDS on a tea estate there (see table at right). The study found that the costs are determined by the levels of both employee benefits and of skilled labor necessary for production. It predicted that, in the longer term, the negative impact on the supply of skilled labor will be the strongest effect of HIV/AIDS.[31] It will become increasingly difficult to recruit skilled people, even at the national level.

TABLE 5.4   **Cost of HIV/ AIDS on a Tea Estate**
Source: Stover and Bollinger 1999

COST OF HIV/AIDS ON A TEA ESTATE IN MALAWI			
Description	Total Cost (£)	Related to HIV (%)	Cost of HIV (£)
Provision of medical services	22,275	25	5,569
Funeral costs	928	75	696
Death in service benefits	4,691	100	4,691
Absence	14,875	25	3,719
Total	42,769		14,675

3. Economic Impact on Firms

HIV/AIDS impacts the business sector by 'increasing expenditures and reducing revenues' (World Bank 1999:16). Many industries are facing up to increased levels of absenteeism and are having to recruit replacement labor as their staff fall sick and die; in turn incurring costs in recruitment, training, health—care, medical insurance, sickness and burial payments (Seghal 1999; Cohen 'time lost to AIDS related sickness' followed by 'healthcare costs' were ranked as the two main impacts of the epidemic on their workforce and business operations (Bloom et al 2000b). 1992: 5; Bloom 1999a; Bloom 1999b). In a recent survey of businesses in thirty African countries,

A specific example of the impacts of the epidemic is provided by the case of a sugar estate in Kenya which calculated the cost of the epidemic as follows:— 'absenteeism (8000 days of labor lost due to sickness between 1995 and 1997 alone), lower productivity (a 50 percent drop in the ratio of processes sugar recovered from raw cane between 1993 and 1997) and higher overtime costs for workers obliged to work longer hours to fill in for sick colleagues' (UNAIDS 2000:31).

Ultimately, resources available to firms – savings — for financing 'capital expenditure' and for expanding will be reduced; the very viability of many firms on the continent is in question. Not only are labor supplies changing, but demands for certain products are likely to be affected as consumers re—prioritize and allocate more of their income to health expenditure (Cohen 1992: 11).

Some sectors are clearly more vulnerable than others to the vicissitudes of the epidemic. Labor intensive industries (for example transport) and those requiring migrant labor (such as mining) are the worst affected as well as sectors employing highly skilled labor since their employees are harder to train and recruit and are fewer in number. For example, Malawi is suffering from losses of skilled water engineers who are very difficult to replace (Topouzis 1998: 25). In these circumstances, the design, construction and maintenance of dams, roads, schools, public health centers, irrigation systems, power stations etc. will be affected given the losses in skilled human resources. Indeed, it has been suggested that a high disease burden – say from malaria or HIV/AIDS— may have adverse indirect effects the rate of technological advance. This is because technological advance depends very much on the level of education and the skills of the labor force. Indigenous innovation and the adaptation of foreign technologies will also depend on the availability of a core of highly skilled scientists and engineers. In an environment that is heavily impacted by disease and where the level of human capital will, as we have noted, tend to be lower, such skills will typically be absent. Moreover, to the extent that technological advancement comes from the direct investment of high technology foreign firms, the very process of technological diffusion may be affected if such investments are deterred by the prevalence of disease. (Sachs, 2000)

National economies are clearly at greatest risk when their principal foreign exchange earning sectors are affected by the disease, for example there is evidence from Kenya that the government's delay in establishing a national prevention policy was driven by the fear of losing its valuable tourist industry (Cohen 1992: 11).

AIDS may have a significant impact on some firms. AIDS—related illnesses and deaths to employees affect a firm by both increasing expenditures and reducing revenues. Expenditures are increased for health care costs, burial fees and training and recruitment of replacement employees. Revenues may be decreased because of absenteeism due to illness or attendance at funerals and time spent on training. Labor turnover can lead to a less experienced labor force that is less productive.

TABLE 5.5   Factors of Expenditure and Revenue

Factors Leading to Increased Expenditure	Factors Leading to Decreased Revenue
Health care costs	Absenteeism due to illness
Burial fees	Time off to attend funerals
Training and recruitment	Time spent on training
	Labor turnover

Source: World Bank,1997

The actual distribution of these costs has been calculated as part of various USAID—funded AIDSCAP studies of the private sector impact of AIDS:

- One study examining several firms in **Botswana** and **Kenya** showed that the most significant factors in increased labor costs were absenteeism due to HIV or AIDS and increased burial costs as shown in the figure to the right.[32]

FIGURE 5.6   Distribution of Increased Labor Costs

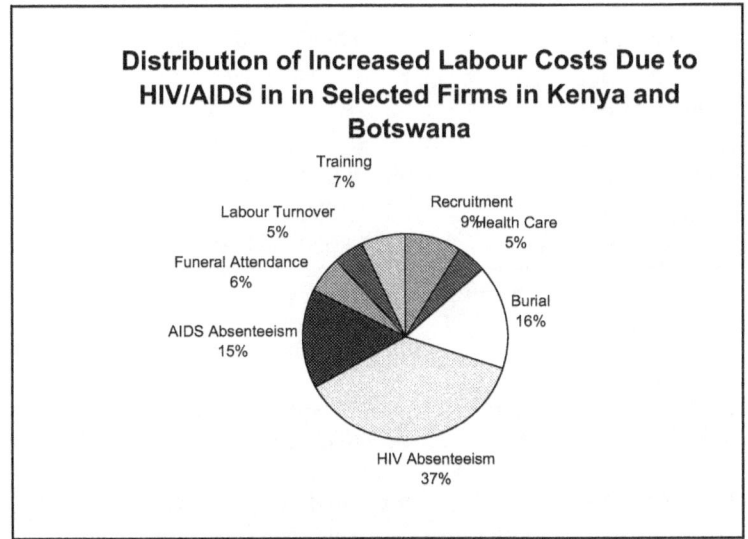

Source: Rugalema et al. 1999

- Another study in **Zimbabwe** shows that the major expense was health care costs. The transport company in this study has a large staff of 11,500 workers. Since the company offers significant health benefits to its employees, the cost of AIDS is even higher than for other companies that do not provide such benefits. The study estimated that there are currently more than 3,400 workers who are infected with HIV and sixty—four who died from AIDS in 1996. The total costs of AIDS to the company in 1996 were estimated at Z$39 million, equal to about 20 percent of the company's profits. More than half of this amount resulted from increased health care costs. By 2005 the cost of AIDS to the company could reach Z$108 million. There may be indirect costs as well. The report speculates that HIV/AIDS will worsen employee morale and create greater labor—management tensions and cause a labor shortage among skilled positions.[33]

Various studies have also examined the total annual cost of AIDS to different companies, as well as the annual cost of AIDS per employee.[34] These studies found that the annual cost of AIDS per employee varied from US$17 to US$300, as shown in the table below:

TABLE 5.6 Cost of AIDS to Companies

Company Name	Total Annual Cost of AIDS	Annual Cost of AIDS per Employee
Botswana Diamond Valuing	US$ 125,941	US$ 237
Botswana Meat Commission	US$ 370,200	US$ 268
Cote d'Ivoire food processing firm	US$ 33,207	US$ 120
Cote d'Ivoire textile firm	US$ 32,667	US$ 29
Cote d'Ivoire packaging firm	US$ 10,398	US$ 125
Kenyan automobile firm	US$ 21,312	US$ 17
Kenyan transport firm	US$ 61,132	US$ 28
Muhoroni Sugar, Kenya	US$ 58,303	US$ 49
Kenyan lumber firm	US$ 40,630	US$ 25
Uganda Railway Corporation	US$ 77,000	US$ 300

Source: Roberts et al, 1997

Increased labor costs can reduce the profits necessary for expansion. This impact on profits can be considerable:

- The Indeni Petroleum Refinery in **Zambia** spent US$26,400 on AIDS—related costs in 1994, more than its declared profits of US$25,514 in that year.[35]
- A study in **South Africa** examined the expected impact of AIDS on employee benefits, and thus on corporate profits. It found that at current levels of benefits per employee, the total costs of benefits would rise from 7 percent of sala-

ries in 1995 to 19 percent by 2005. Since these additional costs will have to be paid at the same time that productivity is declining, due to AIDS, the net impact on profits could be significant.[36]

Finally, other costs associated with AIDS that firms face include:

- The **Uganda** Railway Corporation has been hard hit by AIDS among it employees, experiencing a labor turnover rate of 15 percent per year in recent years.[37]
- Medical aid companies in **Zimbabwe** have estimated that meeting all the claims of just one percent of HIV—infected members could result in a 31 percent increase in insurance rates. Most of this increase would have to be paid by employers.[38]

For some smaller firms the loss of one or more key employees could be catastrophic, leading to the collapse of the firm. In others, the impact may be small. Firms in some key sectors, such as transportation and mining, are likely to suffer larger impacts than firms in other sectors. In poorly managed situations the HIV—related costs to companies can be high. However, with proactive management these costs can be mitigated through effective prevention and management strategies.

4.   Impact on Other Economic Sectors

Health Care

Health care systems – on the front—line in coping with the AIDS crisis – are overburdened by the epidemic and the services that African countries can provide are woefully inadequate (UNAIDS 2000; World Bank 1999). For not only is Africa the worst HIV/AIDS affected region, it is also the world's poorest region with the lowest access to and quality of health care. Health care systems have to deal with increasing numbers of patients with AIDS—related illnesses such as tuberculosis and spending on HIV/AIDS is diverting scarce resources from other major health concerns (UNAIDS 2000: 30; Over 1998).

FIGURE 5.7   Bed Occupancy for Patients in Zimbabwe

Bed occupancy required for AIDS patients, Zimbabwe

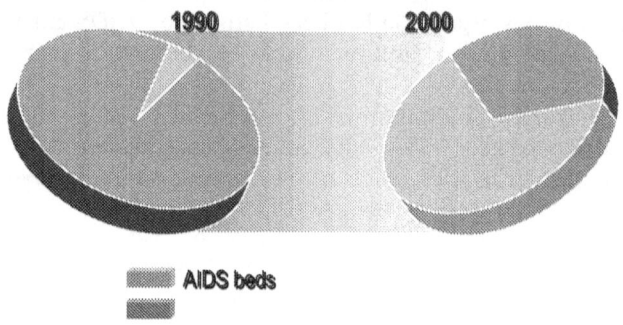

AIDS beds

Source: UNAIDS, 2000

Governments are having to make some harsh choices and are facing trade—offs between: treating AIDS versus preventing new infection; treating AIDS versus treating other illnesses; and spending for health versus spending on other sectors (Bollinger et al. 1999:6).

'In Cote d'Ivoire, Zambia and Zimbabwe, HIV—infected patients occupy 50 to 80 percent of all beds in urban hospitals' and 70% of beds in the Prince Regent Hospital in Bujumbura, Burundi (World Bank 1999: 15; UNAIDS 2000: 29). Not only are beds filling up with AIDS patients but sickness and death is also high among health personnel in some African countries and their skills are hard – sometimes impossible — to replace A study in the Zambia showed that in one hospital, 'deaths in health care workers increased thirteen—fold over the ten year period from 1980 to 1990, largely because of HIV' (UNAIDS 2000: 20).

AIDS will also have significant effects in other key sectors. Among them are health, transport, mining, education and water.

- **Health.** AIDS will affect the health sector for two reasons: Firstly, it will increase the number of people seeking services and secondly, health care for AIDS patients is more expensive than for most other conditions. The number of AIDS patients seeking care is already overwhelming health care systems. In many hospitals in Africa, half of hospital beds are now occupied by AIDS patients. AIDS is also an expensive disease. The graph shows projected expenditure on AIDS as a percentage of public health spending for three African countries.[39] On average, treating an AIDS patient for one year is about as expensive as educating ten primary school students for one year. Governments will face trade—offs along at least three dimensions: treating AIDS versus preventing HIV infection; treating AIDS versus treating other illnesses; and spending for health versus spending for other objectives. Maintaining a healthy population is an important goal in its own right and is crucial to the development of a productive workforce essential for economic development.

FIGURE 5.8   Potential Treatment Costs

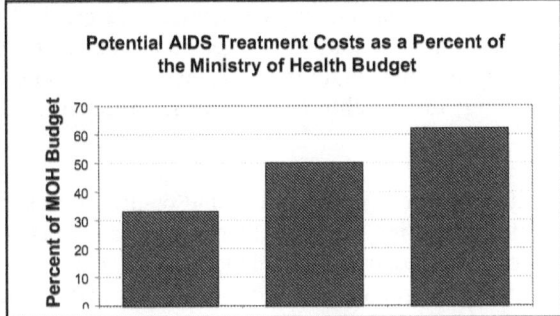

Source: MOH, Ethiopia, Kenya & Zimbabwe, 1998

- **Transport.** The transport sector is especially vulnerable to AIDS and important to AIDS prevention. Building and maintaining transport infrastructure often involves sending teams of men away from their families for extended periods of time, increasing the likelihood of multiple sexual partners. The people who operate transport services (truck drivers, train crews, sailors) spend many days and nights away from their families. A survey of bus and truck drivers in Cameroon found that they spent an average of fourteen days away from home on each trip and that 68 percent had sex during the most recent trip and 25 percent had sex every night they were away.[40] Most transport managers are highly trained professionals who are hard to replace if they die. Governments face the dilemma of improving transport as an essential element of national development while protecting the health of the workers and their families.

- **Education.** AIDS affects the education sector in at least three ways: the supply of experienced teachers will be reduced by AIDS—related illness and death; children may be kept out of school if they are needed at home to care for sick family members or to work in the fields; and children may drop out of school if their families can not afford school fees due to reduced household income as a result of an AIDS death. Another problem is that teenage children are especially susceptible to HIV infection. Therefore, the education system also faces a special challenge to educate students about AIDS and equip them to protect themselves. The education sector, in the hardest hit countries, has been devastated. HIV—related illness takes its toll in a number of ways and teachers, administrators and pupils alike are affected. 'Skilled teachers are a precious commodity in all countries' but in many African countries they are leaving schools and dying at an unprecedented and shocking rate (UNAIDS 2000: 27). The Central African Republic has a third fewer primary school teachers than it needs yet between 1996 and 1998 almost as many teachers died as retired; 85% of them were HIV positive and died on average ten years before the minimum retirement age of 52 (UNAIDS 2000:27). In Zambia, during the first ten months of 1998, 1,300 teachers (equivalent to two—thirds of all new teachers trained annually) were lost to AIDS. The quality of education is undoubtedly affected as class sizes are on the increase and there is evidence that urban—rural disparities in educational access are growing; the psychological damage inflicted is unimaginable.

- **Water.** Developing water resources in arid areas and controlling excess water during rainy periods requires highly skilled water engineers and constant maintenance of wells, dams, embankments, etc. The loss of even a small number of highly trained engineers can place entire water systems and significant investment at risk. These engineers may be especially susceptible to HIV because of the need to spend many nights away from their families.

5.   Macroeconomic Impact

The extraordinary impact of HIV/AIDS on development is attributable to its ability to undermine three main determinants of economic growth, namely physical, human and social capital. (Bonnel 2000) Current estimates suggest that HIV/AIDS has reduced the rate of growth of Africa's per capita income by 0.7 percentage points a year and that for those African countries affected by malaria, growth was further lowered by 0.3 percentage points per year (Bonnel 2000:1). Clearly then, not only is HIV/AIDS having a detrimental effect on the growth of African economies it is reversing the modest gains made in recent times (Over 1992). The effects on growth — at the macro—economic level — are gradual and drawn out over time, partly due to the long incubation period of the virus (Bonnel 2000: Annex 5 : 3).

Broadly speaking we know that poverty, income inequality, labor migration, gender inequality, low levels of education, and a range of context—specific socio—cultural variables and initial health conditions facilitate the spread of HIV/AIDS and are associated with higher prevalence rates (Bonnel 2000)

There is econometric evidence that macroeconomic outcomes are adversely affected by HIV/AIDS (Bonnel 2000:7; Over 1992). The epidemic affects the quality of regulation and the effectiveness of governments as well as a broad range of institutions. The relations between HIV/AIDS and economic development are complicated, for while the disease 'reduces economic growth, economic growth can increase or decrease the spread of the HIV epidemic'. The disease can increase when economic development is associated with inter and intra—national labor migration and investment in large projects (which amplifies local inequalities); and HIV/AIDS can be slowed down if increases in education and employment – particularly female – occur, accompanied by infrastructural developments which facilitate access to health care and safe water (Bonnel 2000:15—16).

HIV/AIDS impacts *physical capital*. The accumulation of physical capital is a function of the savings rate of the economy. It will tend to reduce household saving both in absolute terms and also as a percentage of household income. Moreover, households will likely tend to invest less towards retirement as the expectation of a lower life span takes hold. HIV/AIDS will also impact physical by lowering the volume and uses of domestic savings of governments (Cohen 1992: 4). Budgets are affected by increases in costs associated with treating and caring for AIDS related diseases. Other expenditures, such as pension payments, increase as civil servants are forced to take early retirement. The training of newly hired teachers and health professionals – to replace those lost to the disease — also affects national budgets. Thus, fiscal deficits would tend to worsen generally, as few countries will be able to offset the fiscal cost of the HIV/AIDS epidemic by cutting other expenditures or raising taxes' (Bonnel Annex 5 2000:3). In sum reductions in household and government savings lead to 'less investment, less productive employment, lower incomes and a slower rate of GNP growth, and possibly a lower level of GNP' (Cohen 1992: 4; Over 1992) leading to reduced long—term economic growth.

HIV/AIDS also has an impact on human capital accumulation. As previously noted, HIV/AIDS affects the most economically active age—groups, thereby reducing both the quantity and quality of available labor (Cohen 1992:16; Seghal 1999: 6). Entire generations of teachers, health workers, civil servants and other skilled and professional people are being lost. Shorter life expectancies are raising the costs of schooling and training, thereby reducing the short—term returns (Bonnel, 2000) Since a significant amount of human capital accumulation takes place within the household, the death or sickness of a parent, particularly a mother, can have a disruptive impact on the inter—generational transmission of knowledge. Moreover, children may be forced to leave school to help replace lost income or production caused by the loss of a parent, as family finances come under increasing strain. Thus the *human capital* of African nations is being eroded and incentives to invest in the education training of replacement labor are being reduced (Bonnel 2000, Annex 5: 4).

HIV/AIDS affects not only a country's physical and human capital, but its social capital as well. The epidemic is eroding social networks and traditional support mechanisms as well as challenging the efficacy of legal and regulatory institutions to respond. The quality of countless lives is being eroded and a generation of children are growing up without the emotional and financial support of their parents (Bonnel 2000: 5).

Although the foregoing assessment of the macroeconomic impact of HIV/AIDS provides a a useful summary view of the economic impact of the epidemic. It is perhaps more useful to trace and further explore its impact through some of the context—specific and sectoral transmission modes through which the macroeconomic effects are shaped.

The macroeconomic impact of AIDS is difficult to assess. Most studies have found that estimates of the macroeconomic impacts are sensitive to assumptions about how AIDS affects savings and investment rates and whether AIDS affects the best—educated employees more than others. Few studies have been able to incorporate the impacts at the household and firm level in macroeconomic projections. Some studies have found that the impacts may be small, especially if there is a plentiful supply of excess labor and worker benefits are small. Other studies have found significant macroeconomic impacts. Studies in Tanzania, Cameroon, Zambia, Swaziland, Kenya and other sub—Saharan African countries have found that the rate of economic growth could be reduced by as much as 25 percent over a tweanty—year period.(Stover and Bollinger)

There are several mechanisms by which AIDS affects macroeconomic performance.

- AIDS deaths lead directly to a reduction in the number of workers available. These deaths occur to workers in their most productive years. As younger, less experienced workers replace these experienced workers, worker productivity is reduced. The graph to the right illustrates the magnitude of the problem in five African countries.[41] It shows the increase in mortality among men of working age from the late 1980s to the mid—1990s. Most, if not all, of this increase is due to AIDS.

- A shortage of workers leads to higher wages, which leads to higher domestic production costs. Higher production costs lead to a loss of international competitiveness which can cause foreign exchange shortages.

FIGURE 5.9   **Increase in Mortality**

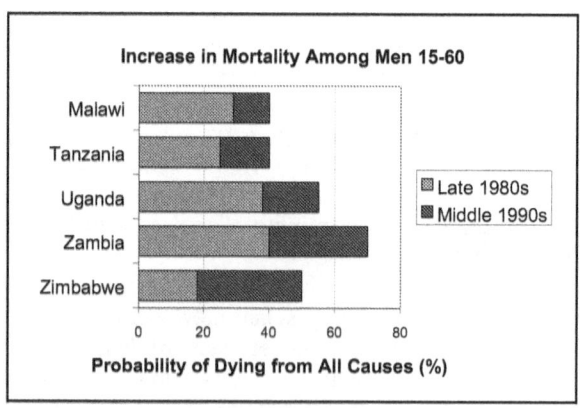

Source: Stover & Bollinger, 1999

- Lower government revenues and reduced private savings (because of greater health care expenditures and a loss of worker income) can cause a significant drop in savings and capital accumulation. This leads to slower employment creation in the formal sector, which is particularly capital intensive.

- Reduced worker productivity and investment leads to fewer jobs in the formal sector. As a result some workers will be pushed from high paying jobs in the formal sector to lower paying jobs in the informal sector.
- The overall impact of AIDS on the macro—economy is small at first but increases significantly over time.

Several studies have found that these effects could be large in some African countries.

- A World Bank study examined the macroeconomic impact of AIDS in thirty sub—Saharan African countries.[42] This study concluded that the net effect is likely to be a reduction of the annual growth rate of GDP of 0.8 to 1.4 percentage points per year and a 0.3 percentage point reduction in the annual growth rate of GDP per capita.

FIGURE 5.10   Reduction in GDP Due to AIDS

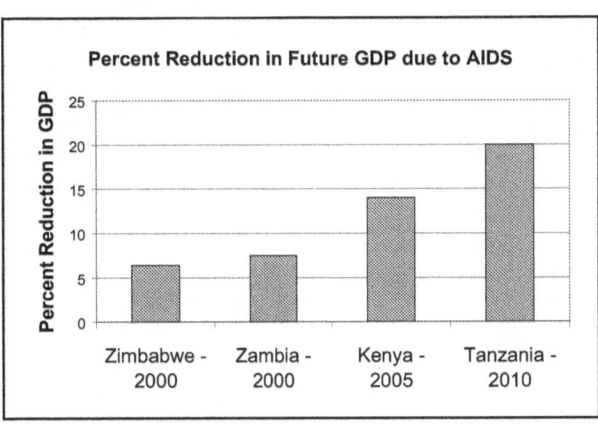

Source: Mead, 1992

- A simulation model of the economy of **Cameroon** concluded that the annual growth rate of GDP could have been reduced by as much as 2 percentage points during the 1987—1991 period because of AIDS.[43]
- A study of the macroeconomic impacts of AIDS in **Zambia** found that by 2000 the GDP would be 5 to 10 percent lower because of AIDS than it would be if there were no AIDS affecting the population. The authors concluded, *"...without unprecedented infusions of free foreign aid to mitigate the effects of AIDS, the economy of Zambia will suffer considerable damage."*[44]
- An assessment of the macroeconomic impacts of AIDS in **Tanzania** by the Government of Tanzania, the World Bank and the World Health Organization in 1991 found that total GDP will be 15 to 25 percent smaller in 2010 because of the impact of AIDS.[45]

- A study of the impact of AIDS on the economy of **Kenya** projected that GDP will be 14 percent lower in 2005 than it would have been without AIDS. GDP per capita will be 10 percent less in 2005.[46]

6. Policy Recommendations for Governments

Finance & Equity

Resources invested in African countries, research institutions and industry ought to be 'drastically increased' (Piot 1998: 1845; Jha et al. 2000). As the Secretary General of the United Nations, Kofi Annan, noted, 'donors — the OECD countries — must make more resources available to fight the epidemic.

At the global level, the 'ultimate challenge for HIV research will be the development of an effective and affordable vaccine. Nevertheless, there is much that can be done at the present time to ensure that the extraordinary scientific progress achieved, in the prevention and treatment of HIV/AIDS, is equitably distributed worldwide (ibid.). The research and development based pharmaceutical industry charges as high prices as the market can bear; their purpose is to maximize profit (Myhr 2000). African countries cannot afford patented (brand—name) drugs and ironically these same drugs are usually more expensive on the African Continent than in wealthier parts of the world. Drugs that are no longer patented may face generic competition and the evidence points to the fact that generics are cheaper (Myhr 2000: 4). Therefore, it is critical that generic drugs are introduced early and that they are widely available and affordable. The pressure is on pharmaceutical companies to face up to their moral obligation and governments (and all concerned parties) to reverse the inequitable pricing and distribution of life—saving drugs.

National Response

At the national level the response should be inclusive, 'such that the epidemic is taken into account when planning or implementing programs in *[all]* sectors that are affected by and [impact] on the HIV/AIDS epidemic (Tarantola 1998: 9). Therefore, national policies ought to be multi—pronged and all ministries should be involved, from health and education to planning and infrastructural development.

The fundamental causes of HIV/AIDS need to be addressed if the epidemic is to be effectively challenged. Long—term structural policy reforms, aimed at combating gender inequality and the economic and social vulnerability of women will be of paramount importance in this endeavor. There is considerable scope for intervention at various levels: the individual, the child, the household and the community (Seghal 1999: 7). Households have to participate in economic growth if they and their communities are to rise out of poverty, 'this means addressing the legal or social constraints which adversely affect the capacity of seropositive individuals from participating in economic activities' (Bonnel 2000: 17; Bollinger et al. 1999).

Governments have much to learn from experiences gained in other African countries and the challenge is to 'incorporate...effective interventions into comprehensive national [programs] (World Bank 1999:18). For example, studies have shown that a combination of voluntary counselling and testing, condom social marketing, peer education and the treatment of sexually transmitted diseases can 'change behaviors and reduce the risk of HIV' (World Bank 1999:17).

7.   Conclusion

In spite of the weaknesses and limitations in existing methodologies and models for measuring the economic impact of disease burdens generally and of the impact of HIV/AIDS in particular, there is sufficient evidence that the overall economic impact of the epidemic is devastating. Indeed the indications are that current estimates based on traditional cost— of— illness studies underestimate the economic impact of the disease.

A full quantification of the overall economic effects of HIV/AIDS on African economies will need to take account of the direct economic effects of adult HIV/AIDS on labor productivity, the economics of childhood HIV/AIDS. It should also take account of changes in household behavior attributable to the disease, as well as changes due to the very risk of HIV/AIDS. Thirdly, it should measure the economic effects at the national level, including effects on the fiscal situation and therefore on the stability of the macroeconomic environment, and effects on enterprise productivity and investments as well as related externalities flowing from lost skills. When all this is done faithfully, the probability is that the economic impact of HIV/AIDS will add up to a lot more than the annual loss of GDP of 2% estimated by the World Bank.

Judging from the sheer scale of these costs, it clear that the return on investment in scaled up efforts at prevention would be enormous. What is required is a comprehensive program for total national mobilization, backed by scientific and technological knows how, significantly enhanced levels of international donor support and improved access to drug therapies. Finally Aids research, including, especially, research by African scientists and institutions ought to be given the highest priority.

AIDS has the potential to cause severe deterioration in the economic conditions of many countries. But this can be stopped. There is much that can be done now to keep the epidemic from getting worse and to mitigate the negative effects. Among the responses that are necessary are:

- **Prevent new infections.** The most effective response will be to support programs to reduce the number of new infections in the future. After more than a decade of research and pilot programs, we now know how to prevent most new infections. An effective national response should include information, education and communications; voluntary counseling and testing; condom promotion and availability; expanded and improved services to prevent and treat sexually transmitted diseases; and efforts to protect human rights and reduce stigma and discrimination. Governments, NGOs and the commercial sector, working together in a multi—sectoral effort can make a difference. Workplace—based programs can prevent new infections among experienced workers.

- **Design major development projects appropriately.** Some major development activities may inadvertently facilitate the spread of HIV. Major construction projects often require large numbers of male workers to live apart from their families for extended periods of time, leading to increased opportunities for commercial sex. A World Bank—funded pipeline construction project in Cameroon was redesigned to avoid this problem by creating special villages where workers could live with their families. Special prevention programs can be put in place from the very beginning in projects such as mines or new ports where commercial sex might be expected to flourish.

- **Programs to address specific problems.** Special programs can mitigate the impact of AIDS by addressing some of the most severe problems. Reduced school fees can help children from poor families and AIDS orphans stay in school longer and avoid deterioration in the education level of the workforce. Tax benefits or other incentives for training can encourage firms to maintain worker productivity in spite of the loss of experienced workers.

- **Mitigate the effects of AIDS on poverty.** The impacts of AIDS on households can be reduced to some extent by publicly funded programs to address the most severe problems. Such programs have included home care for people with HIV/AIDS, support for the basic needs of the households coping with AIDS, foster care for AIDS orphans, food programs for children and support for educational expenses. Such programs can help families and particularly children survive some of the consequences of an adult AIDS death that occur when families are poor or become poor as a result of the costs of AIDS. The costs of these programs can vary widely.[47]

TABLE 5.7   **Annual Cost of Programs to Households**

Annual Costs of Programmes to Mitigate the Household Impacts of AIDS, Kagera, Tanzania, 1992	
Type of Programme	Annual Cost (US$)
Home care for people with AIDS	$227 per patient
Orphanage care	$1,063 per child
Foster care	$185 per child
Feeding post	$69 per child
Basic needs support	$47 per household
Educational support	$13 per child

Source: Stover & Bollinger, 1999

The Spread and Effect of HIV/AIDS in Africa

CHRONOLOGY

The first AIDS cases were discovered in 1981 in homosexual men in United States. The first case on AIDS was reported in central Africa in 1983. It became clear that by 1986 HIV-1 had spread in the populations of many countries in sub-Saharan Africa and had posed a major public health crisis. The discovery of AIDS in African patients who were neither homosexual men nor intravenous drug users led to the realization that AIDS could be transmitted through heterosexual intercourse. This also lead to a shift of paradigm on who gets infected as it was no longer confined to homosexual and intravenous drug users only.

FIGURE 5.11

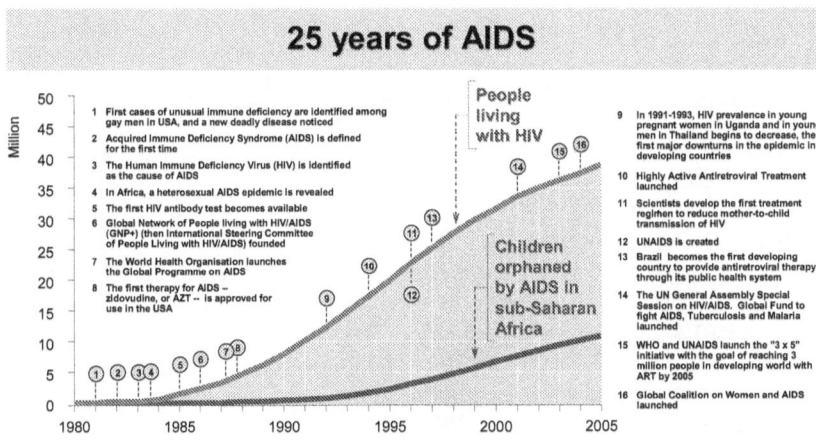

Source: UNAIDS 2006

It has been established that sexual intercourse between men and women results in most HIV-1 infections acquired by adults in sub-Saharan Africa. Evidence suggests that transmission through blood transfusions, injections with infected needles, and scarification are thought to represent only a small amount of infections.

FIGURE 5.12

Adults and children estimated to be living with HIV, 2005

Total: 38.6 (33.4 – 46.0) million

Source: UNAIDS 2006

A notable characteristic of the HIV-1 epidemics in sub-Saharan Africa is their severity. Of the estimated 40 million people who were living with HIV-1/AIDS as the end of 2001, 70% or 24 .5 million are from sub-Saharan Africa, which makes about 10% of the world's population. (Figure1, 2 and 3). According to the UNAIDS/WHO Working Group on Global HIV/AIDS/STI (sexually transmitted infection) Surveillance, an HIV-1 epidemic is generalized if the prevalence in pregnant women repeatedly exceeds 1%. Therefore, in 1999 based on this criteria, the HIV-1 epidemic was generalized in all countries of sub-Saharan Africa with the exception of Mauritania, Somalia, Equatorial Guinea, and the islands in the Indian Ocean. By contrast, in Asia, the second most severely affected continent, three countries had generalized epidemics in 1999: Thailand, Cambodia, and Myanmar.

FIGURE 5.13

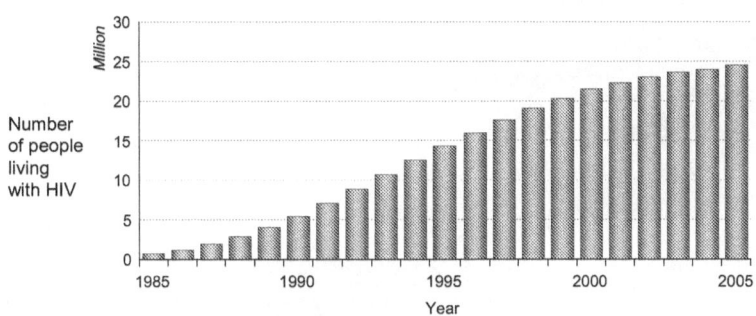

Estimated number of people living with HIV in sub-Saharan Africa, 1985–2005

Source: UNAIDS 2006

Due to the fact that HIV-2 causes much fewer HIV infections in sub-Saharan Africa than HIV-1, in this study we will discuss HIV-1 infection. First, we cover the epidemiology of HIV-1 infection in sub-Saharan Africa. Second, we describe the socioeconomic and cultural implication in which the virus has and continues to spread. Finally, we discuss the demographic effect of the HIV-1 epidemic and the consequences for economic development in Africa.

Epidemiology

The first case of AIDS cases was noted in Uganda and Tanzania shortly after the liberation war in Uganda 1978-79. The AIDS epidemic in the Democratic Republic of Congo began around the same time, although some scientists argue that HIV-1 infection was present in the population long before then. Evidence suggests that the populations of central Africa (figure 1) were the first to have been confronted with the new virus emanates from studies on the virus itself. The HIV-1 epidemics in Cameroon, Gabon, and the Democratic Republic exhibit many circulating HIV-1 strains- more than any other population in the world. This implies that the virus has been present for a long time in these countries. (Figure 5.15) Furthermore, studies indicate that there is a zoonotic transmission of simian immunodeficiency virus (SIV) in Cameroon that gave rise to HIV-1 group N infection in people (UNAIDS,2000)

FIGURE 5.14

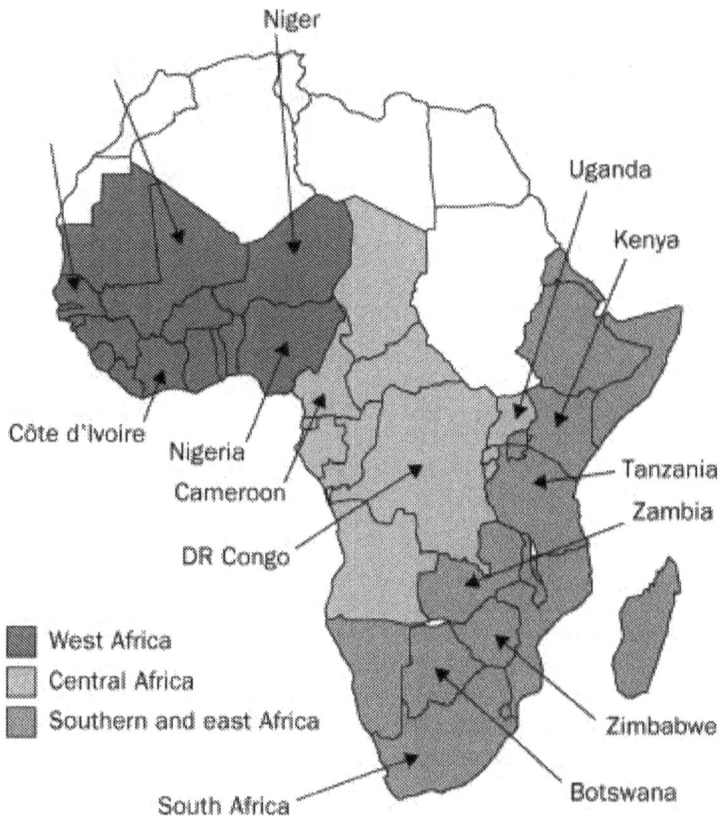

Source: WHO, 2000

In sub-Sahara Africa, antiretroviral treatment is inaccessible and therefore there is still widespread wave of AIDS pandemic. Although the two populous nations of India and China, will determine Asia's final contribution to the pandemic, Africa remains the leader in all aspects of demographic infection despite the fact that Africa has a population of about 600 million(Piot P, Taelman et al 1984) This is approximately 10% of the world's population. Sub-Saharan Africa accounts for over two-thirds of the world's HIV-infected persons, and 80% of the world's HIV-infected women and children. In 1999 alone about 2.6 million AIDS deaths occurred globally and 2 million of them in sub-Saharan Africa. In sentinel populations of pregnant women, HIV prevalence in some parts of southern Africa, such as in Francistown, Botswana, now is greater than 40%. Large variations exist in the severity of HIV/AIDS, the epidemic is concentrated around the eastern and southern parts of the continent. Although prevalence has stabilized in some areas, a stable prevalence implies a high incidence to replace losses due to mortality, and Africa continues to suffer the highest number of new infections witnessed anywhere in the world. The only country that has realized a decrease in HIV prevalence is Uganda, where HIV prevention campaigns since the early 1990s have successfully encouraged abstinence among young people in order to delay the onset of sexual activity and increase condom use . The country currently is experiencing positive results such as in areas where infection rates had reached 40% among pregnant women in cities, HIV/AIDS prevalence in this group is now approximately 15%.(Asimii Okiror, 1997)

FIGURE 5.15

HIV prevalence (%) among pregnant women attending antenatal clinics in sub-Saharan Africa, 1997/98–2004

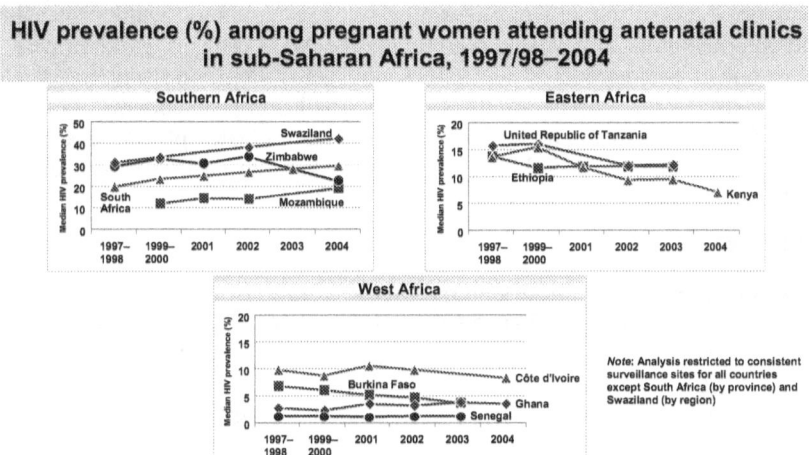

Source: UNAIDS 2006

Explanations for heterogeneities in the epidemic in different parts of Africa must lie in the interaction between the virus, the human host, and the broader environment. The absence of a pandemic of HIV-2, which has essentially remained concentrated in West Africa, is likely to be related to lower transmissibility compared with HIV-1. We have no definitive evidence that important biological differences exist among the various subtypes of HIV-1 in pathogenicity, infectiousness, or predisposition for specific modes of transmission. Subtype A predominates in West Africa; A and D in East Africa, and C in Southern Africa. A recent multicentre comparative study has re-emphasized the role of genital herpes and lack of male circumcision as two of the factors associated with high HIV seroprevalence (Buvéet al. 1999).

3. Public health impact in sub-Saharan Africa

The effects of the epidemic in Africa are obvious across society. HIV/AIDS dominates health structures, rapidly emerging as the leading adult cause of death when
HIV prevalence exceeds a few percent. Across the continent, hospitals are filled
with wasted people. In the shadow of HIV is an epidemic of tuberculosis, the
commonest AIDS-associated illness. Rates of mother-to-child transmission are
higher in Africa than in most industrialized countries, largely because of pro-
longed breast feeding, and infant and child mortality have risen steeply. Increased
peadiatric and adult mortality results in massive reductions in life expectancy,
erasing the gains in health and child survival that have occurred over our lifetimes.
The disability and death of young and middle-aged adults removes families' bread-
winners, providers of school fees , as well as societies' teachers, health professionals and administrators. A new social group are the AIDS orphans, children who
have lost one or both parents to HIV/AIDS, now some 8 million strong in Africa,
raising the specter of a population the size of a small European country of disen-
franchised persons growing up with a bleak future. Associated phenomena are
child-headed households and elderly grandparents caring for different sets of
grandchildren.(Quinn et al 1986)

FIGURE 5.16

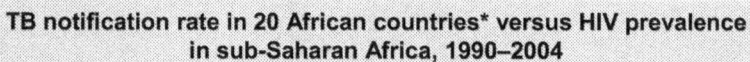

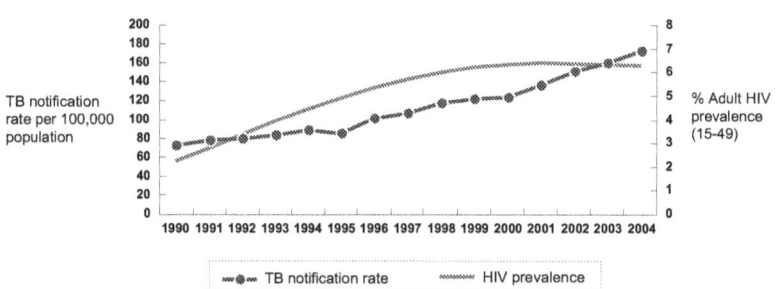

Source: UNAIDS, WHO 2006

Although considerable, the demographic and economic impacts are more obvious
at the local than the macro level. High fertility rates mean it is unlikely that the
population of any country will decline, although population increase is being significantly curtailed. At the level of the local community and especially the family,
however, missing people are only too evident. Similarly, the economic effects of
the epidemic may be hidden at societal level, but vivid to the family which becomes suddenly destitute.

FIGURE 5.17

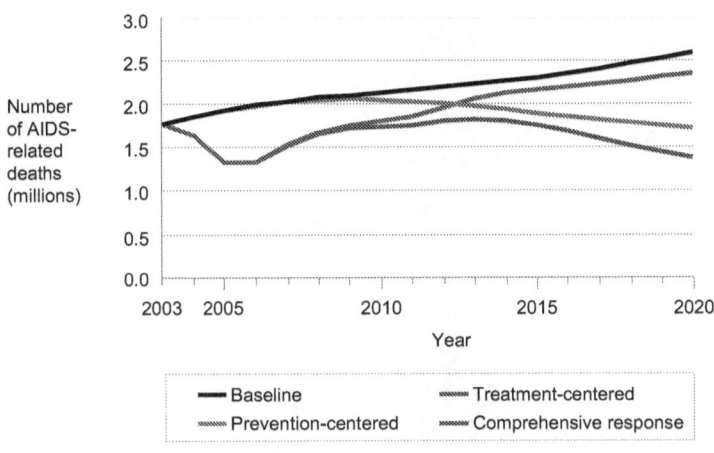

Impact of AIDS-related deaths in sub-Saharan Africa, 2003–2020

Source: UNAIDS 2006

The impact needs to be viewed in its historical and political context. 20–25 million Africans currently living with HIV will die prematurely. For comparison, just over one million Americans have died serving their country in all of America's wars; 800 000 Rwandans died in 100 days of genocide in 1994; from the 14th to 18th centuries, plague is estimated to have killed 25 million people worldwide, approximately the number of Africans currently waiting to die from HIV. (Figure 7) HIV/AIDS is clearly Africa's greatest social catastrophe of the 20th century, its greatest calamity since the slave trade. The impact and duration of the epidemic in the 21st century remain speculative (Quinn 1986).

In the mid-1980's, the HIV-1 epidemic seemed worst in the Democratic Republic of Congo and Uganda, and, to a lesser extent, in neighboring countries in east and southern Africa. In the Democratic Republic of Congo, Cameroon, and Gabon, HIV-1 prevalence has remained fairly stable for many years and only recently has a worrying increase in prevalence in Cameroon suggested that the epidemic is entering a new phase. In 1999, HIV-1 prevalence in adults in Cameroon was estimated at 7.7%; in 2000, a prevalence of 11% was noted in a nationwide

FIGURE 5.18

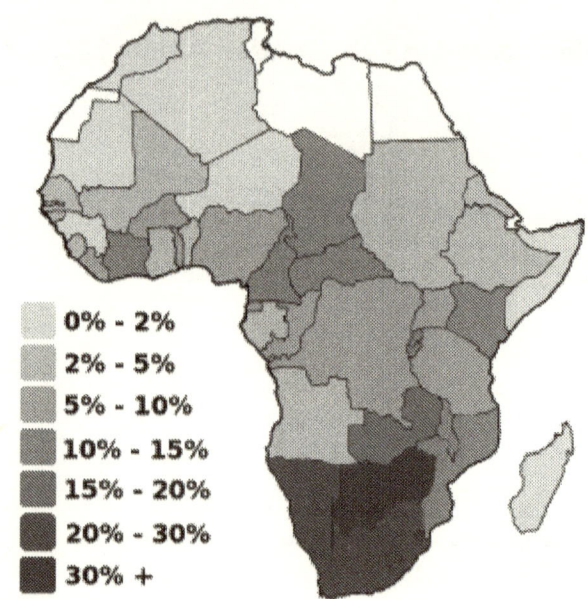

0% - 2%
2% - 5%
5% - 10%
10% - 15%
15% - 20%
20% - 30%
30% +

Source: UNAIDS, 2004

survey of pregnant women. This relatively slow and recent increase contrasts with the situation in many parts of east Africa and most of southern Africa where the HIV-1 epidemic has run an explosive course since the early 1990's (table figure 5.19). In many large cities in these regions, HIV-1 prevalence in pregnant women has exceeded or still exceeds 25% (UNAIDS 2000, Macaulay IB, 2001).

FIGURE 5.19

	Median HIV prevalence (%) among women attending antenatal clinics 2003–2004*	Population-based survey prevalence (%) (year)	2003 HIV prevalence (%) reported in 2004 Report on the global epidemic	Adjusted 2003 HIV prevalence (%) in current report	2005 HIV prevalence (%) in current report	Trend in prevalence
Botswana	38.5	25.2 (2004)	38.0	24.0	24.1	Stable
Burkina Faso	2.5	1.8 (2003)	4.2	2.1	2.0	Decline in urban areas
Burundi	4.8	3.6 (2002)	6.0	3.3	3.3	Decline in capital city
Cameroon	7.3†	5.5 (2004)	7.0	5.5	5.4	Stable
Ethiopia	8.5	1.6 (2005)§	4.4	(1.0–3.5)	(0.9–3.5)	Decline in urban areas
Ghana	3.1	2.2 (2003)	3.1	2.3	2.3	Stable
Guinea	4.2	1.5 (2005)	2.8	1.6	1.5	Stable
Lesotho	28.4	23.5 (2004)	29.3	23.7	23.2	Stable
Rwanda	4.6	3.0 (2005)	5.1	3.8	3.1	Decline in urban areas
Senegal	1.9	0.7 (2005)	0.8	0.9	0.9	Stable
Sierra Leone	3.0	1.5 (2005)	-	1.6	1.6	Stable
South Africa	29.5	16.2 (2005)	20.9	18.6	18.8	Increasing
UR Tanzania	7.0	7.0 (2004)	9.0	6.8	6.5	Stable
Uganda	6.2‡	7.1 (2004–5)	4.1	6.8	6.7	Stable

Adult (aged 15–49 years) HIV prevalence (%) in countries in sub-Saharan Africa which have conducted population-based HIV surveys in recent years

* WHO Africa (2005). HIV/AIDS epidemiological surveillance report for the WHO African region, 2005 Update. Harare
† Estimate based on country report for 2002 (2003). Ministry of Public Health Cameroon. National HIV sentinel surveillance report 2002.
‡ Estimate based on country report for 2002 (2003). Ministry of Health Uganda. STD/HIV/AIDS surveillance report. STD/AIDS control programme. Kampala
§ Preliminary result. Additional analysis is ongoing.

Source: UNAIDS 2006

In Uganda, the prevalence of HIV-1 infection has fallen since the early 1990s, which has been attributed to changes in sexual behavior. More recently, a similar, declining trend in HIV- prevalence has been noted in Zambia. However, in other parts of southern Africa the epidemic continues to spread unabated (figure 3). The worst affected country so far is Botswana, where an estimated one in three adults are infected. In west Africa, with the exception of Cote d'Ivoire, f Burkina Faso, Nigeria, and Togo, HIV-1 prevalence in pregnant women has so far remained under 5% (UNAIDS/WHO 2006).

FIGURE 5.20

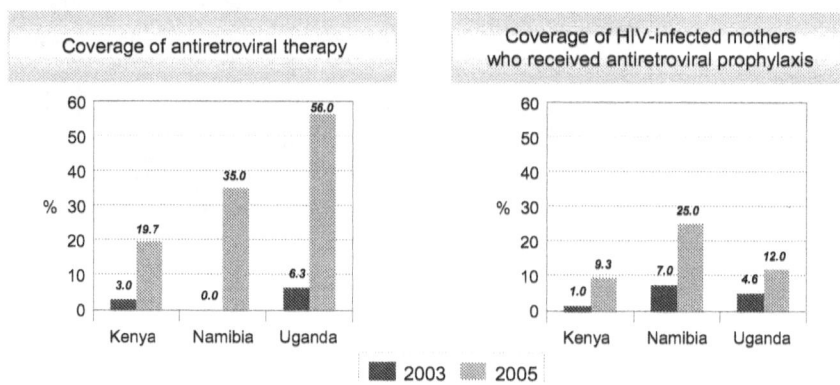

Comparison of 2003 and 2005 data on the expansion of antiretroviral therapy and coverage of HIV-infected mothers who received antiretroviral prophylaxis in three sub-Saharan African countries

Source: UNAIDS 2006

4. Heterogeneity of the Disease

The considerable variation in HIV-1 prevalence between different regions in sub-Saharan Africa cannot always be accounted for by differences in the date of intro-duction of the virus. The rate of spread of HIV-1 infection varies between popula-tions across Africa. Indeed, it seems that the spread of HIV infection has been more rapid in eastern and southern Africa than in Western and Central Africa (ta-ble and figure 2). In population-based study, differences in sexual behavior pat-terns alone could not explain differences between areas in HIV-1 prevalence. The study was done in four cities: two (Cotonou in Benin and Yaounde in Cameroon) with a fairly low prevalence of HIV-1 of around 5% in the general population; and two (Kisumu in Kenya and Ndola in Zambia) with a prevalence of around 25%. Differences in sexual behavior were outweighed by differences in the prevalence of factors that alter the probability of transmission during sexual intercourse, male circumcision and infections that cause genital ulcerations, ie, herpes simplex vi-rus-2 (HSV-2) infection, syphilis, or both. Furthermore, differences in prevalence were not explained by variations in circulating subtypes of HIV-1. The findings show how the spread of HIV-1 infection is determined by a complex interplay of sexual behavior, including rate or partner change and sexual mixing patterns be-tween different sexual activity classes, different age groups, or both, and biologi-cal factors that affect the probability of HIV-1 transmission per sex act (Buve, Carael, Hayes).

FIGURE 5.21

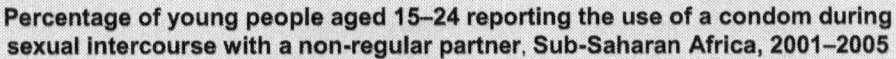

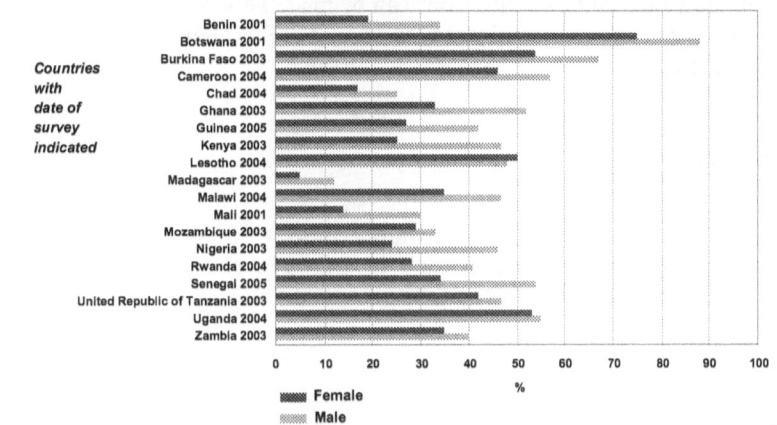

Source: UNAIDS 2006

The study also drew attention to the high prevalence of HIV-1 and other sexually-transmitted infections in young people, especially young women, in many parts of sub-Saharan Africa. For instance in Kisumu, Kenya, 23% of women aged 15-19 years were infected with HIV-1, compared with 3.5% of young men of the same age. Female adolescents in Tanzania, Zambia, Zimbabwe, and South Africa have much higher rates of HIV-1 infection than male adolescents. Possible explanations for this discrepancy include the higher biological vulnerability of young women to HIV-1 and other sexually transmitted infections than young men, and sexual relations between young women and older men who are more likely to be infected than younger men. Indeed, sex with older men is a risk factor for HIV-1 infection in young women in Zimbabwe, Further work is needed on the sexual behavior of young people and the biological factors that make young women more susceptible to HIV-1 infection, such as cervical and HSV-2 infection. Meanwhile, the HIV-1 epidemics in sub-Saharan Africa could clearly be stemmed only if the prevalence of HIV-1 infection falls in young people, especially young women (Laga, Sow 2001)

5. Why is sub-Saharan Africa more severely affected than other continents?

By the end of 2001, the HIV-1 prevalence in adults in sub-Saharan Africa was estimated at 8.4%. Estimated prevalence rates on other continents did not exceed 1%, apart from the Caribbean region, where it was 2.2%. No comparative be-tween-continent data exists on sexual behavior and other risk factors for HIV-1 infection. However, some comparisons can be made between sub-Saharan Africa and southeast Asia, the subcontinent with second highest number of people living with HIV-1 infection.

FIGURE 5.22

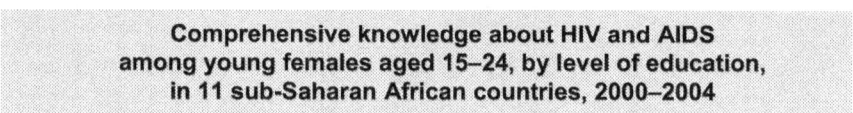

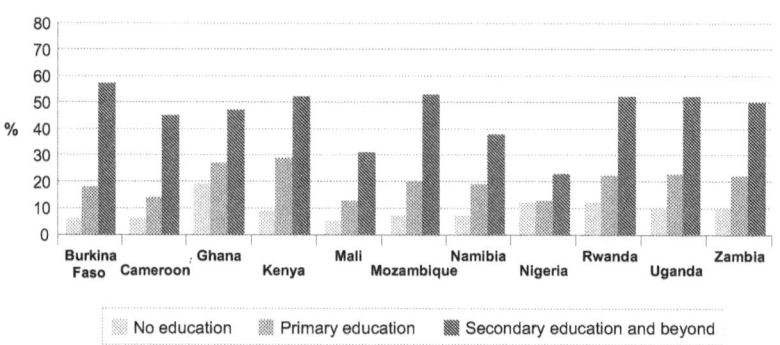

Source: UNAIDS 2006

Although HIV-1 epidemics in most parts of Africa started about 10 years earlier than in southeast Asia, this factor is unlikely to fully account for the differences in HIV-1 prevalence between the regions. For instance, the HIV-1 epidemics in South Africa and Thailand both began in the early 1990's but by 1999, HIV-1 prevalence in the general population was 19.9% in South Africa and 2.2% in Thai-land. Yet, the population of many parts of Africa and of southeast Asia have at least one risky sexual behavior pattern in common such as sex between men and sex workers (Sittiral, Brown 2006).

FIGURE 5.23

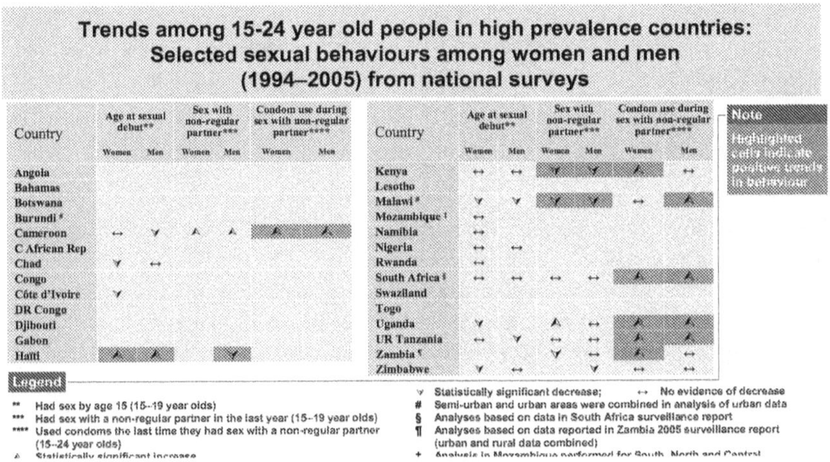

Trends among 15-24 year old people in high prevalence countries: Selected sexual behaviours among women and men (1994–2005) from national surveys

Country	Age at sexual debut**		Sex with non-regular partner***		Condom use during sex with non-regular partner****		Country	Age at sexual debut**		Sex with non-regular partner***		Condom use during sex with non-regular partner****		
	Women	Men	Women	Men	Women	Men		Women	Men	Women	Men	Women	Men	
Angola							Kenya	↔	↔				↔	
Bahamas							Lesotho							
Botswana							Malawi#	↓	↓			↔		
Burundi#							Mozambique+	↔						
Cameroon	↔	↓	↑	↑	↑	↑	Namibia	↔						
C African Rep							Nigeria	↔	↔					
Chad	↓	↔					Rwanda	↔						
Congo							South Africa§	↔	↔	↔	↔			
Côte d'Ivoire	↓						Swaziland							
DR Congo							Togo							
Djibouti							Uganda	↓		↑	↔			
Gabon							UR Tanzania	↔	↓	↑	↔			
Haiti	↑	↑			↑		Zambia¶			↓	↔			
							Zimbabwe	↓	↔		↓	↔	↔	

Note: Highlighted cells indicate positive trends in behaviour

Legend

** Had sex by age 15 (15–19 year olds)
*** Had sex with a non-regular partner in the last year (15–19 year olds)
**** Used condoms the last time they had sex with a non-regular partner (15–24 year olds)
↓ Statistically significant increase

↓ Statistically significant decrease; ↔ No evidence of decrease
Semi-urban and urban areas were combined in analysis of urban data
§ Analyses based on data in South Africa surveillance report
¶ Analyses based on data reported in Zambia 2005 surveillance report (urban and rural data combined)
+ Analysis in Mozambique performed for South, North and Central

Source: UNAIDS 2006

In a multi-center study of factors determining different prevalence of HIV-1 in sub Saharan Africa, the portion of men who reported at least one contact with a sex worker in the past year ranged between 3% in Kisumu and 12% in Yaounde, but these figures are thought to be grossly underestimated. In a nationwide survey in Thailand, 24.2% of men in Urban and 9.5% in rural areas reported paying for sex in the previous year; male sexual behavior on Cambodia follows a similar pattern(Glynn, Auvert et al 2001)

There are, however, important differences between southeast Asia and sun-Saharan Africa. Large-scale interventions to promote condom use with sex workers, which were supported at the highest political level, were initiated earlier in the course of the HIV-1 epidemic in Thailand and Cambodia than in most of sun-Saharan Africa. In Bangkok, Thailand in 1996, 97% of sex workers based in brothels and 78% of indirect sex workers (such as beer girls) reported consistent condom use with all their clients. In Cambodia, interventions were started later than in Thailand, but by 1999, 78% of sex workers based in brothels reported consistent condom use with all their clients. In sub-Saharan Africa in 1997, only 28% of sex workers in Yaounde and Ndola, 50% in Kisumu, and 69% in Cotonou reported condom use with their most recent client.

However, the extent of the spread of HIV-1 in the general population is not only determined by unprotected sexual intercourse between sex workers and their clients, but also by the extent to which male clients of sex workers have intercourse with female partners who are not sex workers who in turn have sex with several other male partners. According to available data, women in sun-Saharan Africa have premarital sex with several partners more often than do women in southeast Asia. Therefore, the high HIV-1 rates in young women, which are driving the HIV-1 epidemics in sub-Saharan Africa, are unlikely to be seen in southeast Asia. These high rates may, however, change if young women in southeast Asia change their sexual behavior, because of a changing socio-economic context (Carael, 1995)

6. Socioeconomic and cultural context

Cultural and socioeconomic features common to most societies in sub-Saharan Africa have played, and still play, a part in the spread of HIV-1 infection. These factors include the subordinate position of women in society, impoverishment and the decline of social services, and rapid urbanization and modernization. To this gloomy picture must be added the many wars and conflicts in Africa. Since 1980 at least 28 of 53 African states have engaged at war.

7. Gender roles and the Subordinate position of African women
Social and cultural systems in many African societies dictate that women have no control over their sex lives, or the sex lives of their husbands outside marriage. Extramarital affairs by both sexes are tolerated in many parts of sub-Saharan Africa, but most cultures have rules requiring women to have very little sexual experience before marriage and to be monogamous thereafter, whereas for men premarital and extramarital sex are tolerated or even expected. Young men and boys are often encouraged by peers to demonstrate their masculinity through early sexual initiation and many sexual conquests. Bride payments- financial compensation to a bride's family by her new husband-perpetuates the idea that a woman is her husband's property. This culturally prescribed lack of control on their sexual relationships has made women, particularly married women, highly vulnerable to HIV-1 infection. Wives are not allowed to refuse sex from their husband, or to use a condom, even if the husband is infected with HIV-1. The subordinate position of women also has implications for safe-sex education. Men are supposed to know everything and cannot admit ignorance, whereas women are not supposed to be aware of issues related to sex. (Ferry, Buve et al 2001)

FIGURE 5.24

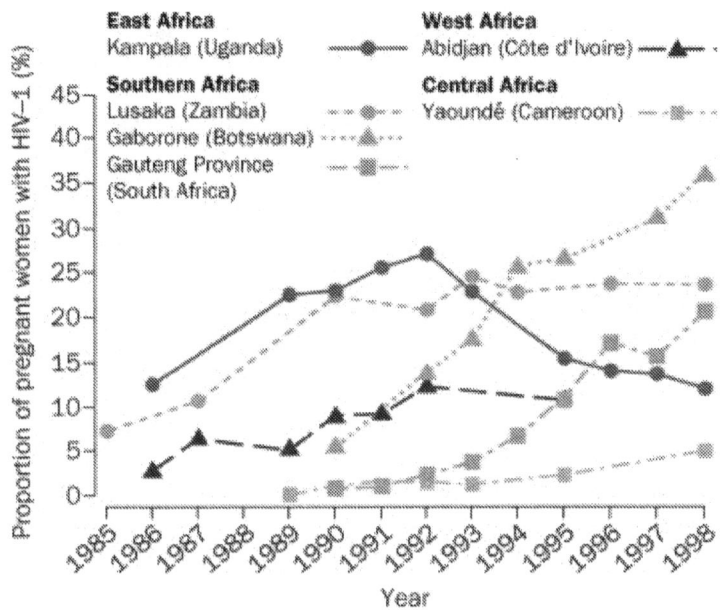

Source: US CENSUS BUREAU 2000

The gender power differential is compounded by age differences and the economic dependence of women on men. Women typically marry have sex with older men. In a multi-center study, the median age difference between spouses, reported by women, was 6-7 years. Furthermore, young married women in Kisumu and Ndola had a higher risk of HIV-1 infection if their husband was more than 3 years older than themselves.

Women face restrictions such as discriminatory laws, traditions, and values when they try to access education, knowledge, land, capital, and employment. As a result, women are economically dependent on their male partners, which makes negotiation of safe sex difficult. For unmarried women and women who are widowed or separated, sex in exchange for money can be a strategy for survival or acquisition of goods. In a multi-center study, 40% of women in Kisumu and Ndola who reported non-spousal partnerships in the previous year, reported sex in exchange for money or gifts; the corresponding figures for Cotonou and Yaounde were 6% and 14%, respectively. Most of these women were unmarried and could not be termed sex workers.

8. Poverty and decline of social services

During the past 20 years, nearly all countries in sub-Saharan Africa have faced showing economic growth. Between 1980 and 1991, the average yearly growth of per capita gross national product in sub-Saharan Africa was -1.2%. Structural-adjustment programs imposed cuts in non-productive spending, including spending on social services. This policy further impoverished African populations, with increases in unemployment resulting from privatization of public enterprises and loss of jobs in the public sector. The remaining public sector workers saw their purchasing power diminished. Additionally, the provision of social services lessened, including education and health services. Thus, during the 1990's overall public expenditure on health represented only 1.7% of the gross African domestic product.

Poverty is associated with increased vulnerability to HIV-1 and other sexually-transmitted infections. In conditions of poverty, the risk of HIV-1 infection assumes low priority among people's daily concerns. Young people who grow up in poor conditions have little access to schools and few prospects for their future. They lack recreational facilities and sex becomes a way to pass time. Poverty can also drive women into exchanging sex for money, food, or other commodities. Poor people in rural areas migrate to towns in search of work, leaving their family and entering an environment where sexual risk-taking is more common than in their rural homes. However, the association between poverty or wealth and the risk of HIV-1 infection is not straightforward. Higher educational attainment can be associated with more risky sexual behavior and increased risk of HIV-1 infection in individuals, which was true especially in the early stages of the HIV-1 epidemic. At the population level, there is no simple link between per capita gross national product and the prevalence of HIV-1 infection. Botswana, Namibia and South Africa have the highest per capita gross national product in sub-Saharan Africa, but are the hardest hit by HIV-1. Mead over identified eight epidemiological, social, and economic variables that could account for more than half the variation in HIV-1 prevalence between 72 countries in Africa, Asia, and Latin America. Per capita gross national product was one variable, but also important were inequality of income distribution and the gap between male and female literacy (UNAIDS 2005)

FIGURE 5.25

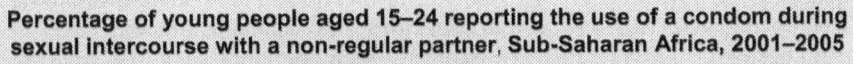

Percentage of young people aged 15–24 reporting the use of a condom during sexual intercourse with a non-regular partner, Sub-Saharan Africa, 2001–2005

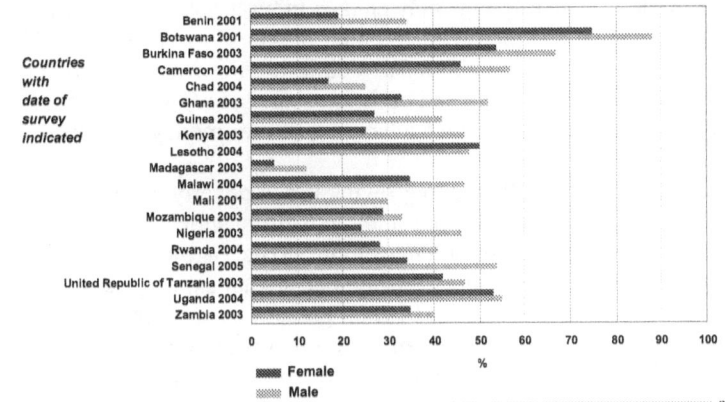

Source: UNAIDS 2006

The decline of health, education, and other social services implies a loss of opportunities for HIV-1 prevention. People with little or no education have poor access to safe-sex information. For instance, condom use is associated with higher levels of education. Reduced provision of quality health services also represents a loss of opportunities to control other sexually-transmitted infections, offer reproductive health services, and provide quality care for people infected with HIV-1, For instance, in Mwanza region, Tanzania, fewer than 10% of symptomatic sexually-transmitted infections occurring in the population were cured by health services. Health staff had been unable to update their skills and knowledge, and health centers were provided with insufficient and inappropriate antibiotics(UNAIDS, 2006)

9. Urbanization and Modernization

The rapid growth of urban areas in developing countries, resulting from increased urban birth rates and continued migration from rural regions, has fuelled the rapid spread of HIV-1. In most parts of sub-Saharan Africa, HIV-1 prevalence is higher in urban then rural populations, which is one reason who some highly urbanized countries have the highest rates of adult HIV-1 infection (figure 4). Urbanization and modernization exchange traditional village norms for an urban modern ethos with fewer restrictions on sexual behavior and marriage. Part of the night urban prevalence of HIV-1 infection results from massive migration of young, unmarried adults from conservative rural environments to more sexually permissive cities. Furthermore, loss of culture and erosion of social networks are associated with social problems such as drug abuse, which encourages high-risk behavior(WHO, 2006)

Migration to urban areas in search of employment separates spouses for extended periods. Urban men and women who are separated from their spouses are more likely to engage in high-risk sexual behavior than cohabitants in urban areas. For many decades, rural migrants have typically been young men aged 15-30 years, especially in Africa. Male migrants may engage in high-risk behavior with sex workers, thereby increasing their own and their partners' vulnerability to HIV-1 and other sexually-transmitted infections. Women are now increasingly migrating to cities. These women frequently end up in low-status, low-wage production and service jobs, and may be forced into exchanging sex for money or gifts as survival strategy.

Rapid urbanization has been linked to growing urban poverty, since jobs are scarcer than applicants. Results from a study in Nairobi showed that slum residents initiate sex at younger ages and have more sexual partners then other city residents. Additional qualitative data showed that sexual exposure and behavior of slum residents were strongly affected by their precarious economic and social conditions. Under the population pressure of rapid urbanization, city infrastructures can collapse and health services deteriorate with concomitant loss of opportunity to prevent the spread of HIV-1(WHO, 2005)

Modernization has brought higher mobility. Better communication and transportation now link urban and rural areas economically and socially. Inter-country and intra-country population mobility has been a critical factor in the spread of HIV-1 in many regions. Key population groups that are highly mobile and at a high risk of HIV-1 transmission are sex workers, truck drivers, transport workers, the military, mobile employees of large industries, and seafarers. Occupational travel is associated with high rates of partner change, transactional sex, and unsafe sex. Travelers thus play a part in bridging epidemics between areas of high and lower HIV-1 prevalence.

FIGURE 5.26

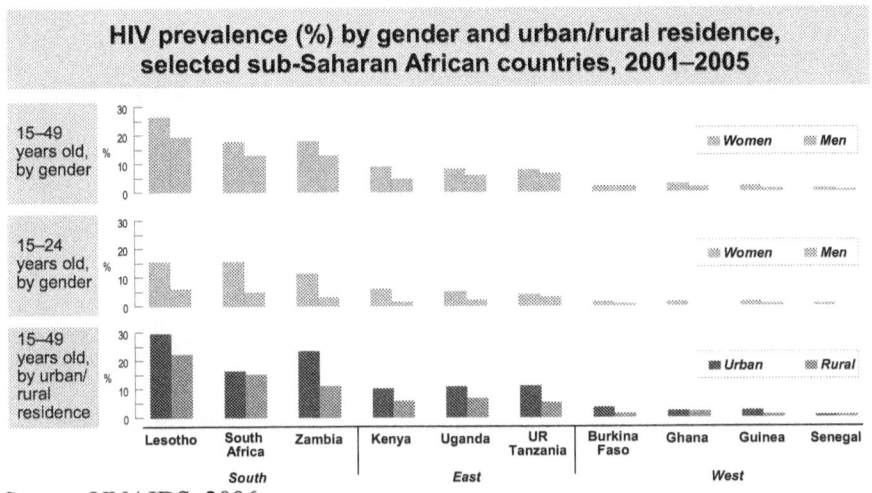

Source: UNAIDS, 2006

10. Wars and Conflicts

War and civil strife are conductive to the rapid spread of HIV-1. During conflicts, soldiers are living in high-risk environment in which risk of HIV-1/AIDS is balanced by stressful situations and dangers related to war. Civilians are often subjected to human rights abuses, including sexual violence, and are left in conditions of poverty that might lead them to use commercial sex to survive.

Additionally, war and civil strife are associated with massive displacements of people. In January, 2002, more than 6 million people in sub-Saharan Africa fell under the mandate of the United Nations Commission on Refugees (UNHCR). Displacement is associated with interruption of social cohesion and relationships, promiscuity, inadequate shelter, and commercial sex. People may also flee from areas with quite low HIV-1 prevalence to an area with a higher prevalence. In Kigali (Rwanda) in 1995, the prevalence of HIV-1 in pregnant women originating from rural areas was higher than displacement during the genocide(Cohen, 2000)

11. The demographic and economic effect of AIDS in Africa

The HIV-1 epidemics in sub-Saharan Africa are causing profound changes in the population structure in more severely affected countries, mainly as a consequence of high mortality in adults and children younger than 5 years. In community-based studies in Tanzania and Uganda, the adult mortality attributable to HIV-1 infection was 35-47% in Tanzania and 69-74% in Uganda. In south Africa, where the HIV-1 epidemic is of more recent onset, the Medical Research Council estimates that in the year 2000, 20% of all deaths in adults were due to HIV-1/AIDS. In rural Botswana, Zimbabwe, and South Africa, life expectancy has been estimated to fall from 60 years in 1990, to about 30 years by 2010(World Bank, 2005)

TABLE 5.8

Summary of studies of the macroeconomic impact of HIV/AIDS in Africa

Study	Countries (period of economic data)	Period of most recently used HIV/AIDS data	Results (comparison with non-HIV/AIDS scenario)
Dixon et al (2001)[5]	41 countries (1960-98)	Late '90s	Growth rates reduced by 2-4%; large variation across countries, in line with prevalence of HIV
World Bank (2001)[10]	Swaziland	Early '90s	Average rate of growth of GDP in 1991-2015 will be 1.5% lower a year
World Bank (2001)[11]	Namibia	Early '90s	Average rate of growth of GDP in 1991-2015 will be 1.1% lower a year
World Bank (2000)[12]	Lesotho	Late '80s	Average rate of growth of GDP in 1986-2015 will be 0.8% lower a year
Bonnel (2000)[13]	About 50 countries (1990-7)	Mid-'90s	Rate of growth of GDP per capita reduced by 0.7% a year in the 1990s
Quattek et al (2000)[14]	South Africa	Mid-'90s	Average rate of GDP growth over next 15 years will be 0.3-0.4% lower a year
BIDPA (2000)[15]	Botswana	Late '90s	Average rate of growth of GDP in 2000-2010 reduced by 1.5% a year
Bloom et al (1995)[16]	51 countries (1980-92)	Early '90s	Insignificant effect on income growth
Cuddington et al (1994)[17]	Malawi	Early '90s	Average rate of growth of GDP in 1985-2010 reduced by up to 0.3%
Cuddington (1993)[18][19]	Tanzania	Early '90s	Per capita GDP in 1985-2010 up to 10% smaller
Over (1992)[20]	30 sub-Saharan countries	Early '90s	Rate of growth of GDP per capita in 1990-2025 reduced by 0.15% (0.6% in 10 worst affected countries)

Source: BMJ. 2002 January 26; 324(7331): 232–234.

These high mortality rates in young adults inevitably have an economic effect. The effect of AIDS in households is quite well documented through case studies. AIDS-related illness and death leads to deepening poverty. Furthermore, one of the first actions taken by households to cope with the crisis to take children out of school, therefore jeopardizing their future. However, the macroeconomic effect of

AIDS is difficult to assess. The macroeconomic effect depends on how the epidemic affect savings and investment rates and whether AIDS affects better-educated employees more than others. A review of published work does not provide a clear picture of the economic effects of HIV-1/AIDS in Africa because of methodological variation in inclusion of effects at household, company, and civil society levels. Some studies predict negligible macroeconomic effect of HIV-1/AIDS in countries with a high unemployment rate, whereas others predict significant effects on growth rates. In Malawi, for example, the yearly loss in per capita gross domestic product as a result of AIDS is estimated to reach 0.7% by 2010 World Bank 2006)

FIGURE 5.27

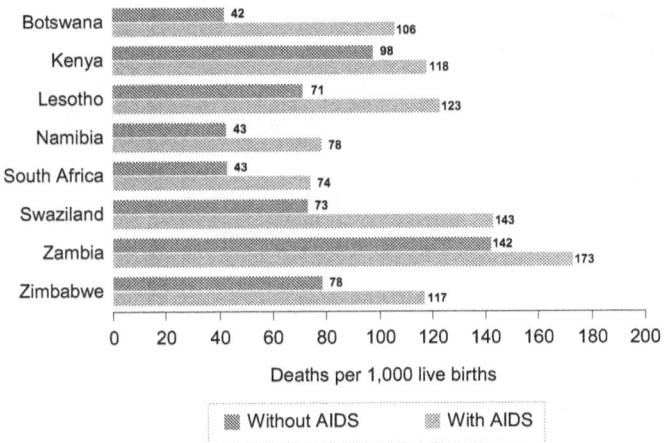

Estimated impact of AIDS on under-five mortality rates 2002–2005, selected countries in sub-Saharan Africa

Source: UNAIDS 2006

FIGURE 5.28

Impact of orphanhood on school attendance among 10–14-year-olds (%)

	West (9 countries)	Central (6 countries)	Eastern (9 countries)	Southern (10 countries)	All (34 countries)
Percentage in school					
Non-orphans	67	75	70	88	74
Orphans	58	69	54	84	69
Double orphans	57	58	49	80	64
Ratios					
Double vs. non-orphans	0.86	0.94	0.72	0.90	0.87
Boys	0.96	0.96	0.82	0.93	0.94
Girls	0.91	0.94	0.88	0.96	0.93

Source: UNAIDS 2006

A more useful indicator of the effect of AIDS might be the human development index, which is used to measure achievements in basic human development. The composite index includes life expectancy at birth, education, and adjusted per capita income. For example, Zambia had a lower index in 1997 than in 1975, largely as a result of the effect of HIV-1/AIDS on life expectancy.

FIGURE 5.29

Life expectancy over time

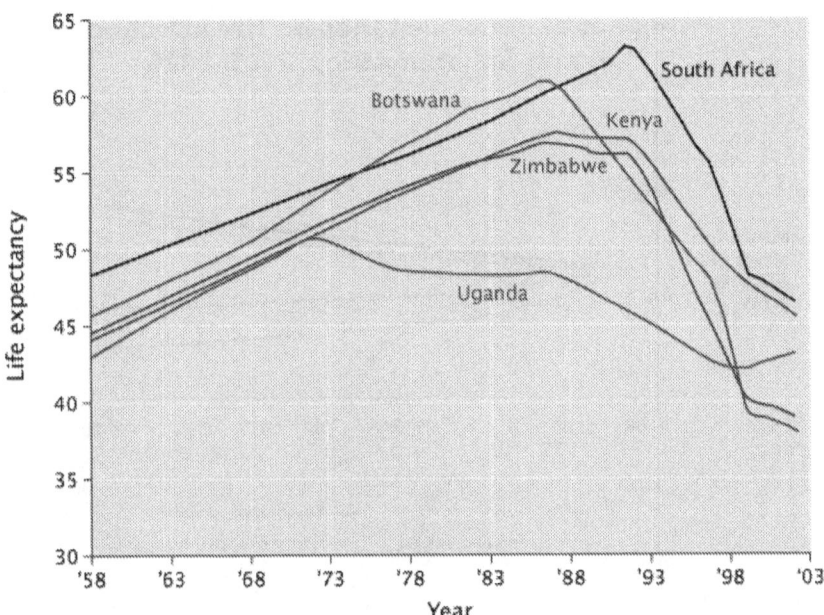

(Source: World Bank *World Development Indicators,* 2004).

Conclusion

HIV-1 epidemics in sub-Saharan Africa are the result of a complex interplay of behavioral factors and factors that affect the transmission of HIV-1 during sexual intercourse, including other sexually-transmitted infections and male circumcision. Sexual behavior patterns are determined by cultural and socioeconomics contexts, some of which have contributed to the extensive spread of HIV-1 infection. When designing prevention strategies, interventions should not only target individuals, but also aim to change the aspects of these contexts that increase vulnerability to HIV-1 of people and communities.

Traditional gender roles in most sub-Saharan Africa enhance the vulnerability to HIV-1 of both women and men. Men and women must work to counter gender discrimination and subordination of women. Central to this process is the full participation of all generations. Law and policy makers, community leaders, and other people in positions of power should recognize the connection between women's economic and social status and their vulnerability to HIV-1 infection. The importance of equal participation of women in identification of interventions and decision-making processes cannot be overemphasized.

FIGURE 5.30

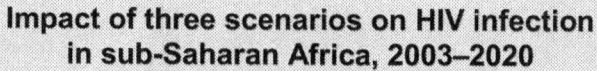

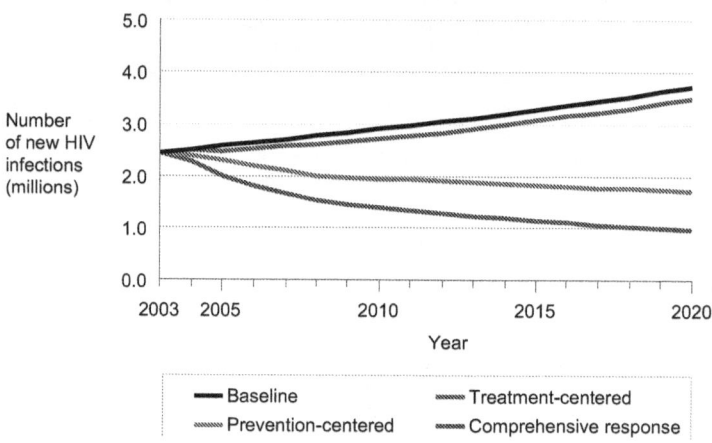

Source: UNAIDS 2006

The impoverishment of African populations and the many wars and conflicts on this continent constitute a fertile ground for the spread of HIV-1. The epidemics in their turn worsen poverty and jeopardize the future of young generations. Families and communities cannot cope with the many orphans who are left uneducated and with an uncertain future. Until the problem of economic development in Africa is tackled, convincing young people to adapt their sexual behaviour to secure their future will remain difficult. The recent renewed international attention for the HIV-1/AIDS epidemics in sub-Saharan Africa should translate to a commitment to reconstruct social services, especially education and health services, and to tackle economic underdevelopment (UNAIDS, 2006)

ECONOMETRIC MODEL OF NEOCLASICAL SOLOW GROWTH

An attempt to examine the impact of human capital on economic growth using an econometric framework can be found in Mankiw, Romer and Weil (1992). Their framework augments the standard Solow growth model by explicitly incorporating human capital as an additional factor of production. They assume that aggregate output in country i and time t, Y_{it}, is a function of physical inputs K_{it}, labor L_{it}, labor-augmenting productivity A_{it}, as well as human capital E_{it}:

$$Y_{it} = \left(K_{it} \right)^{\alpha} \left(E_{it} \right)^{\beta} \left(A_{it} L_{it} \right)^{1-\alpha-\beta} \qquad (5.1)$$

Where α and β are the elasticities. Mankiw et al. (1992) conceptualize human capital solely as educational attainment and do not incorporate health in their empirical estimation. A subsequent paper by Knowles and Owen (1995) extends their framework by incorporating both education E_{it} and health H_{it} as components of human capital:

$$Y_{it} = \left(K_{it} \right)^{\alpha} \left(E_{it} \right)^{\beta} \left(H_{it} \right)^{\psi} \left(A_{it} L_{it} \right)^{1-\alpha-\beta-\psi} \qquad (5.2)$$

As mentioned in the previous section, there are several reasons to include health as an input of the macroeconomic production process. Health is directly correlated with labor productivity. In addition, healthier populations-due to lower health-related expenditure and higher probabilities of future survival-are more likely to save and invest for the future. Health, in addition to providing utility in itself, also influences the ability of individuals to gain utility from consumption of other products. Interestingly, in their empirical estimates Knowles and Owen (1995) find a strong, more robust relationship between health capital and income per capita than between education capital and income per capita(who, 2006)

1. Incorporating HIV as accumulation of Health Capital

The most appealing and apparent way to incorporate HIV/AIDS into the augmented Solow model is following the approach taken in Dixon, McDonald, and Roberts (2001) and in McDonald and Roberts (2004). This approach assumes that HIV/AIDS prevalence has an effect on the accumulation of health capital. In addition to an aggregated production function, it specifies a second equation characterizing a health production function, whereby health outcomes in a country are assumed to be a function of several inputs. These inputs z_{it} could be taken to include factors such as health expenditure, infrastructure, governance, education, etc. Health outcomes are also assumed to be functions of a country's epidemiological environment d_{it} (such as disease prevalence rates):

$$H_{it} = f \left(z_{it}, d_{it} \right), \qquad (5.3)$$

By taking the HIV prevalence rate to be a proxy measure for d_{it} we can estimate its impact on macroeconomic growth through its effect on health capital accumulation.

We use the share of gross domestic product (GDP) invested on average over each 5-year period (I) as a share of resources devoted to physical capital. Education capital accumulation E is the secondary school enrollment ratio. For health capital H, as Anand and Ravallion (1993) and others followed, using the shortfall of life expectancy (LE) from 70 years, defined as ln (70-LE).

The equation estimated:

$$\ln(YC) = f\left[\ln(I), \ln(n+g+\delta), \ln(E), \ln(YC_{-1}), \ln(H)\right] (5.4)$$

Where:

YC = Real GDP per capita
 I = Share of GDP invested
 n = Population growth rate
 g = technological growth rate
 δ = Depreciation rate of capital
 E = Secondary school enrollment
 H = Life expectancy shortfall
HIV = Prevalence of HIV
MAL = Population at risk of malaria
CAL = Calorie intake per capita

The model incorporates endogenous health capital. We instrument it in a two-stage estimation procedure.

Thus we have the following health production function:

$$\ln(H) = f\left[\ln(YC), HIV, \ln(MAL), \ln(CAL)\right], \qquad (5.5)$$

The predicted value is used as an independent variable.

TABLE 5.9

Estimation Results Sub-Sahara Countries

	Full Sample $i = 60; n = 30$
Dependent variable : ln (YC)	
ln *I*	.126
ln *n+g+δ*	.161
ln E	-0.021
ln (YC.₁)	.665
Predicted in *H*	.234
Constant	1.578
HIV Impact	-.054

Dependent variable: ln H	
ln (YC)	.124
HIV	-0.24
ln MAL	-0.215
ln CAL	.275
Constant	-6.370

The coefficients of the regression estimates are depicted on Table 2. Malaria has negative sign indicating the adverse health effects of widespread prevalence of the disease. Calorific consumption has significant positive effect on life expectancy. HIV/AIDS has a strong negative effect of life expectancy. The overall impact of HIV/AIDS prevalence on income per capita can be derived from coefficients and is estimated to equal to -0.054. This indicate that one percent point increase in the HIV/AIDS prevalence will decrease income per capita by 5.4%.

2. Summary of the model

This summary details the derivation of the econometric model, data used, estimation strategy, as well as detailed results. The production function is specified as:

$$Y_I = \left(K_{it}\right)^{\alpha} \left(E_{it}\right)^{\beta} \left(H_{it}\right)^{\psi} \left(A_{it} L_{it}\right)^{1-\alpha-\beta-\psi} \qquad (5.6)$$

Rewriting this in terms of quantities per effective unit of labor:

$$y_{it} \left(k_{it}\right)^{\alpha} \left(e_{it}\right)^{\beta} \left(h_{it}\right)^{\psi}, \qquad (5.7)$$

Where y=Y/AL, e=E/AL, and h=H/AL. Assuming a constant function of output is saved and invested, labor grows at a country-specific rate n_i; technology grows at a period-specific rate g_t; and all forms of human capital depreciate at the same date δ for all countries yields the equation for the steady-state output per capita y_{it}^*:

$$Ln \quad y_{it}^* = +Ln \quad A_{i0} + g_t t - C_1 \quad Ln\left(n_1 + g_t + \delta\right) + C_2$$
$$Ln \quad s_i^K + C_3 \quad Ln \quad s_i^E + C_4 \quad Ln \quad s_i^H \qquad ,(5.8)$$

Where
$$C_1 = \left(\alpha + \beta + \psi\right)/\left(1 - \alpha - \beta - \psi\right),$$
$$C_2 = \alpha/\left(1 - \alpha - \beta - \psi\right), \quad C_3 = \beta/\left(1 - \alpha - \beta - \psi\right), \qquad (5.9)$$

and $C_4 = \psi / (1 - \alpha - \beta - \psi)$. s_i^K, s_i^E, and s_i^H (5.10)

are the shares devoted to physical, education, and health capital, respectively. A_{i0} is the initial level of technology in country i. Linearizing around the steady-state level of output per capita, we get the following two equations. The first is in terms of growth in output per capita, and the second in terms of levels of output per capita:

$$Ln \; y_{it}^{*} - Ln \; y_{i0}^{*} = \varphi Lny_{i0}^{*} + \sum_{j} \theta_j x_{it}^{j} + \eta_t + \mu_i + v_{it}, \quad (5.11)$$

where
$$\varphi = 1 - e^{\lambda t}, \theta_1 = -\theta_2 = \varphi\alpha / (1-\alpha), \theta_3 =$$
$$\varphi\beta / (1-\alpha), \theta_4 = \varphi\psi / (1-a), x_{it}^{1} = Ln(n_i + g_t + \delta),$$
     (5.12)

$$x_{it}^{2} = Ln \; s_i^{K}, x_{it}^{3} = Ln \; e_{it}^{*}, x_{it}^{4} = Ln \; h_{it}^{*}, \text{ and } \eta_t = g_t t. \; \lambda$$
     (5.13)

is the convergence rate. The same equation can be written in terms of levels as well:

$$Ln \; y_{it}^{*} = (1-\varphi) Ln \; y_{i0}^{*} + \sum_{j} \theta_j x_{it}^{j} + \eta_t + \mu_i + v_{it}. \quad (5.14)$$

This is becomes the equation that forms the basis for estimating the effects of human capital on economic growth.

VI. Summary and Conclusion

This study has analyzed the determinants of poverty in Kenya. Prior to the analysis we gave the definition of poverty. The study defined poverty in terms of minimum rural household income. The minimum income used is the amount necessary for a Kenyan rural household to meet basic needs annually.

Using the minimum income criteria this study and past studies concluded that nearly 60 percent of the Kenyan rural population were living below the defined poverty line. This was the major reason we decided to investigate and identify the major causes of poverty in Kenya so that a solution be sought to alleviate it.

The study identified the key variable causes of poverty as; prices of food crops, government expenditure on public investments in agricultural sector, rural household income, essential imports, export prices and quantities, area of land cultivated for export crops and the amount of labor used in the export crop sector.

The analysis began by showing us the conceptualized frame work of the study. Within this framework we identified the structural characteristics of Kenyan economy resembling a small open country economy. The implication of this identification is that Kenya cannot influence the prices of her exports. Therefore Kenya is a price taker in selling her exports. As such, the international price of exports and imports, which influence the rural household income, are exogenously determined whereas domestic producer prices are affected both exogenously and endogenously by foreign demand of agricultural products and the rate of surplus extraction by the government. This leads to an increase in poverty.

The survey provided us with a theoretical analysis of the peasant agricultural economy as a typical case a Kenyan farmer faces on economic decision making. The literature we reviewed is based on the theory of the optimizing peasant in regards to decisions of what to produce, how to produce, how much to produce and for whom. In this case the price plays a dominant role and the farmer is very sensitive to the price changes and profitability. The literature on crop expansion showed that the farmer maximizes the value of total output subject to technological constraint. This was ascertained empirically in our results. Maximization of crop output can be achieved through an increase in crop expansion thus shifting the farmer's production frontier outward.

The field study was undertaken in Kenya in order to find out the structure of the rural economy. The field survey was carried out by use of a questionnaire. The questionnaire was deliberately designed to provide us answers on the relative importance of various crops, the market orientation of farmers, the constraints on production and the degree of diversification. The answers to this questions provided us with basis for making policy implications on poverty alleviation. It was shown that the proportion of farmers growing a given crop is generally a useful indicator of the relative importance of that crop to the economy. The results show that for the country as a whole, the most widespread food crop was maize then followed by vegetables, beans and milk. This is true because a typical Kenyan diet comprises all these crops.

We also found out that prices and other monetary incentives play a dominant role on farmers who are in the money economy. The study found out that coffee, tea and pyrethrum are only grown for sale. These can be termed cash crops because they are not for consumption at home but for sale. It was noticed that when the prices increase farmers increased the export crops. As far as food crops are concerned we found that production was only for subsistence aimed at satisfying their own demand. We can conclude that in each area of Kenya there exist a cash crop and a subsistence crop.

We found out that traditional Kenyan agriculture uses no inputs from outside the agricultural sector. The study found out that the major constraint on agricultural production was credit followed by capital. Capital in this case is a subsistence fund that the farmer needs in order to maintain his family and laborers during the months when his crops are not yielding any revenue. Labor became a constraint only when marginal revenue of agricultural output is so low that it is uneconomic to increase output by hiring more labor. In this case labor shortage reflected itself as capital shortage when willing farmers lack the financial resources to use in hiring more labor and do not have access to credit facilities.

We found out that farmers in Kenya give higher priority on growing food crops than cash crops. We also noticed that the proportion of farmers selling their produce in any class bears a high positive correlation to the proportion of their total output which is sold. On the contrary, the less important an export crop to the area, the less likely the farmers in that area specialize in that food crop's production. The study found out that 90 percent of all the farmers investigated specialize in food production. The findings conclude that farmers in general were diversified in crop production. The high degree of diversification is due to farmer's desire to minimize fluctuation in their incomes because crops are affected differently by weather conditions. Another explanation of the high degree of diversification is the small sizes of rural markets and its unreliability in supplying foodstuffs. We found out that the farmers' high premium on self sufficiency in food production is consistent with our theory of the peasant agricultural economy detailed in the literature review.

On the whole, the results of the field survey indicate that our model in the literature review is quite realistic with respect to its assumptions about peasant farmers in Kenya. We also found out that monetary incentives do not play a total factor in food production but other factors contribute which we discussed in the literature review on the theory of the optimizing peasant in chapter III.

The study also found out that the size of agricultural production and the level of prices act as determinants of the population living below the poverty line. This helped to give the following major reasons why poverty was not alleviated:

The important role played by international and domestic prices. That is, the international prices of Kenyan tradeable commodities and the prices of importables.

The price of foreign imports is based on border price criterion. This is the world price at free on board exports, at cost, plus insurance and freight for imports, when it is all converted into domestic currency at the official exchange rate. This border price typically needs to be adjusted to bring into comparison with domestic prices like retail, wholesale and/ or farm—gate prices. When adjusted to the farm—gate, we obtain both export and import prices.

The role of government intervention creates multiple markets and prices. The government uses taxes and transaction costs to influence prices in both the informal and formal sectors and creates two markets with different prices. Price of food crops in the formal market depends on the official consumer price of food crops minus the marketing cost of the official agency.

There are differing natures of domestic markets for food and export crops that must be realized.

The size of overall agricultural output, induced by the pattern of public investment, is linked to technological change in agriculture that is fundamental to the achievement of overall increase in output as well as to the alleviation of poverty. What this means is, if the expenditures were directed towards agricultural technology, then rural transport and communications, education and training of the rural entrepreneurial class, and the production of rural commodities would increase. If the government increases spending on technological change in the export crop sector, then this would result in an increase in import capacity. This allows an increase in importation of essential inputs which are needed in export crop sector.

The domestic prices are influenced by international demand and the extent of net extraction of revenue by the government. The latter influences levels of poverty through its effect on both prices and public investment. This in turn can determine levels of agricultural output and avert market failures through investments in transport infrastructure, which increases factor and product mobility directly. The relative importance to be attached to technological change and other investments in two sectors should depend on marginal returns to investments in particular crops. This is so because agriculture contributes more than sixty percent of the GNP. It is the public expenditure patterns that determine the extent to which these revenues, extracted by the government from the agricultural sector, should be siphoned back to agriculture for future production.

Through a simple model the study identified the structural characteristics of the Kenyan economy as resembling those of a small open agricultural country economy. The study then outlined the role of international and domestic demand of food crops and the size of agricultural production in influencing the incidence of poverty in Kenya we argued that the major determinants of Kenyan poverty are the quantities of agricultural tradeable commodities relative to the prices of importable essentials and the domestic producer of price of food crops and export crops. The size and composition of agricultural production are a function of the various relative prices and investment in the agricultural sector. The basic model we used to estimate poverty in the linear model identified rural income, price food and government expenditure on public investment technologies as the independent variables.

The results of government revenue indicated that there is an inverse relationship between an increase in government on agricultural public investments and reduction of poverty. This confirmed our hypothesis we stated that there exist an inverse relationship between increase in government expenditure on technical change and poverty alleviation. Therefore, due to this finding, the government should increase the expenditure on public investment in agricultural technologies.

We ran the regression analysis and we got the following results. The coefficient of rural income was negative and significant telling us that increase in rural income will lead to a reduction in poverty. The rural household income is a function of the price and quantities of food crops, and the price and quantities of export crops. In this case the study recommended policies that would lead to improvement of the above variables so rural household income will increase, thus reducing poverty.

The coefficient of actual price of food was positive that increase in the price of food will reduce poverty. This is so because the beneficiaries of the increase in the price of food are the rural households. The goodness of the fit of the model was ninety eight percent in explaining poverty. The study decided to maximize rural household income because it was highly significant. In the alternative model, exports became the dependent variable because of our finding earlier that it plays a role in sixty percent of the Kenyan gross national product. Secondly, exports played a key role as a component of rural household income. The study identified the independent variables in terms of exports as actual prices of food, essential imports, actual quantities of food, amount of land used in export crops, amount of labor used in the export crop sector and government expenditure in technology on the export crop sector.

The essential imports are inputs such as spare parts, machinery, pesticides and fertilizers needed in the export crop sector. The coefficient on essential imports was positive indicating that increase in essential inputs used in the export crop sector will lead to an increase in quantity of exports. This in turn will lead to an increase in rural household income thus minimizing poverty. The policy we recommend is that the government should subsidize the importation of essentials so that it leads to both farmers' low cost of production and higher profitability. This will lead to the maximization of rural household income and the minimization of poverty. The government should deliberately implement a policy that would increase the quantity of essentials, which in turn would lead to an increase in exports to maximize rural household income and minimize poverty.

The coefficient of actual price of food is negative indicating an inverse relationship between exports and an actual price of food crops. This means an increase in price of food leads to decrease in exports. In this case we recommended that the government should subsidize the actual price of food so that its price falls thus leading to an increase in exports.

The study found that the coefficient of actual quantities of food is positive telling us that increase in actual quantities of food leads to an increase in exports thus leading to maximization of rural household income and minimization of poverty.

The coefficient of land was negative indicating a negative relationship between the increase in the cultivated land and the reduction in exports because the land exhibits diminishing returns. The study concludes that increase in the cultivated land does not play a major role in the alleviation of poverty because of low significance test.

The policy implication we analyzed did not take into account the specific situation of women in agricultural sector. Women play a dominant role in the agricultural production in Kenya, and yet the policies that have been implemented do not include women activities. Thus, we can conclude based on our findings that the high participation of women in the agricultural sector and the low implementation of policies which address these women is a form of exploitation of women by the society. The ideological roles that women are subjected to are partly to blame for this situation. Therefore, despite the policy recommendation we have suggested for the maximization of rural household in income, these policies will directly impact the situation of women.

The reason women have been put in this condition is due to the traditional and ideological reasoning prevalent in Africa today. This condition has denied women their share of the pie although they contribute sixty to eighty percent of making the pie. We also argued that women can not attain the target level of poverty alleviation unless this stumbling block is eliminated by proper policy that deliberately directs resources to those who contribute most. The benefits accrued from rural households should go directly to women.

We explained that the justification that is given in these societies is that women take pride in this role. We included the findings of Ester Boserup who found out that more women than men were usually working more hours per week in agriculture. Boserup also found out that women performed eighty percent of total agricultural production including both food and cash crops.

The justification of womens' roles as providers was given as that they were fulfilling their societal role and they were proud of it. Bryson also found out similar findings concerning women's exploitation. Bryson's finding concluded that women take considerable pride in their agricultural work and derive personal satisfaction from their productivity. This conclusion concerning women has been found to be false and the study recommended a policy that will consider women's wishes and contribution in the agricultural sector.

Abundant empirical evidence suggests that women's access to agricultural resources have been constrained by men's domination of resources that leads to efficiency losses in production. Beneria has added that the justification of this exploitation is ideological and is associated with the tendency to regard women's work as secondary and subordinate to that of the men. The other ideological bias originates from the conceptualization of the role played by women at different levels of economic life. The study recommended that there is a need to reconstruct these concepts in such a way that the role of women in society can be placed in its proper perspective.

The study recommended that there is a need for policies that are based on equitable distribution of resources so that women can get a fair share of revenue thus leading to poverty reduction in the whole section of the society. The first policy is to channel essential inputs to women and to allow women to have access to land rights which have been denied due to the ideological reasons we described earlier in our findings in policy implications. This will allow women to exercise their sovereignty in making economic choices rather than being confined to subsistence production only.

Also, the traditional positioning of women within the farm should be eliminated so that women can exercise their right to work anywhere within the farming system. The study also recommended that the division of labor based on gender should be eliminated because it is not based on ability.

The study found that AIDS is a current impediment to economic development in sub—Saharan Africa. We found out that HIV/ AIDS affects people in their productive years, thus robbing Africa of the human capital necessary to help them grow.

There is a need to educate the people about infection and the consequences of the disease in society. The government needs to invest in community programs that will inform especially the more vulnerable groups. If the people are made aware of the disease, then they will be able to protect themselves.

HIV/ AIDS is a disease that can be controlled. By changing especially the sexual behavior, the consequences of AIDS can be reduced. If the disease is not curtailed, the African productive population will be severely handicapped and the result will affect GDP and the whole structure of African economies.

The suburban model on AIDS depicted the variables affected by AIDS as investment, employment, and agricultural output. This model can be used to simulate HIV/ AIDS impact on these key variables, according to each country's individual scale of HIV/ AIDS.

This study has explained the determinants of poverty for sub—saharan Africa in the agricultural sector. It has laid the groundwork for greater insight and further research.

Appendix A

THE FIELD SURVEY

The relative importance of food crops and export crops are the most significant variables within agricultural sector in most parts of Kenya. These variables are heterogeneous. It consists of peasant farmers for whom agriculture is not wholly a commercial activity but a way of life as well as an activity for whom market exchange is not only dominant but essential for livelihood. Despite language differences which impedes communication and huge disparities in weather conditions, nevertheless farming practices vary little across the country. One contributing factor was the uniformity of government policies, which all the farmers are subject to.

Several strata were identified. One consisted of areas where exports are most important: Muranga, Kiambu, Kericho, Nandi, Nyeri etc. The second strata was where intermediate importance. The third strata consists of Northeastern districts where exports are not grown at all. The main production in this area is livestock mainly for home consumption and exchanged in the local economy. Exports and imports in this strata is between the government and the other districts, whereby supply and demand is based on beef products and basic commodities. The fourth was identified as the strata with only food crops plays a dominant role. These are identified as Uasin Gishu, Tranzoia, Kitale, Nakuru, Kajiado, and Narok. All samples were taken from small villages in each district. No urban centers in each district were actually sampled.

Selection of Villages

The selection of villages was not done on random basis. This was due to resource and time limitations that could not allow us to cover all areas in the country. This made the sample smaller than expected but the selection was careful in order to achieve a very representative of the desired study. Because of past experiences, other areas of the districts could not be included due to farmers not cooperating with the researchers from University of Nairobi in the past. In some instances farmers did not trust us because they could not express themselves since we might be government agents.

Most of the selection was done after extensive discussions with some University of Nairobi agricultural economists whom I had worked with and had contacts there and knew the areas very well. The others were selected after discussions with agricultural extension officers. The general procedure was to ask what villages in the respective districts would cooperate and give us the information we request. They would show us if we wanted to see the best farmers of that area.

Selection of Farmers

In some villages, it was necessary to give advance notice of the visit which interviews actually took place; in other words it was not necessary. We quickly found out that giving advance notice substantially increased our efficiency in terms of time. We therefore made it part of the regular procedure in most villages we visited.

We started by seeking out the chief in each village. He in turn organized a village meeting where we explained our mission and purpose of the study. Such explanations were necessary in order to allay villagers suspicion and fears, especially of taxation. In general, reporting farmers were completely enumerated, except for those who lived under the same roof. Also, we found that in most villages a household do not comprise the nucleus family but includes all those who eat from the same pot are considered one family. The rationale for including those who live under the same roof is because they be working together on the same set of farms, as frequently happens between father and son and sometimes among brothers or other relatives. Where the number of farmers appeared too large for a complete enumeration, every other farmer was interviewed in the first instance and then the process was repeated with the remaining farmers.

A word is vital about the representative ness of reporting farmers. It would appear at first the sample would heavily biased in favor of those farmers who fear, respect, or otherwise obey the village head.

However, the village headman is not particularly powerful position as such, and he does not generally enjoy any particular privileges that might distort his standing among villagers. Therefore, the village head role is leadership that is needed to communicate any important news of general interest and is responsible for organizing meetings. It is in the interest of each farmer thus to attend these meetings whenever they are called. One may conclude that the village meetings assemble a representative if not a complete sample of the farming population of each village.

Enumeration

The farmers were interviewed, on an individual and private basis, sometimes in their houses, sometimes in their farms and most often outdoors in the villages. They were encouraged to give answers only if they understood the questions and had answers to them and to say they did not know if indeed they did not know.

The actual enumeration was done during the period of July 25, to August 19, 1996. Five experienced enumerators assisted on a full time basis. Rather than allocate enumerators among several villages at the same time, the entire team worked together on one village and moved to the next when their job was finished. Similarly, each village cluster was completed before the next one was started. In this way, the enumerators supervision was direct, with the result that there were no frequent problems of enumerators turning in schedules for fictitious farmers.

Beyond Randomness

Although, only rather token attempts were made to randomize the sample the survey should not be evaluated on the basis of the randomness of the sample alone. Its primary purpose was to answer the questions raised in the statement of the problem and in the model specification and to contribute to our scant knowledge of the peasant agricultural economy. If its findings turn out to be of interest, the problem of investigating their degree of representativeness and estimating parameters more efficiently could be taken up as a separate project.

Appendix   B

FARMER INTERVIEW SCHEDULE

Introduction

This questionnaire is designed to obtain information about agriculture in Kenyan rural farmers that will be helpful in developing policies and programs for promoting more rapid increases in output and improvements in farmers' standard of living and consequently poverty alleviation. It is also intended to find out how trade between export and food and commodities and domestic domestic markets interact. Neither names nor facts for individual farmers will be made available to any other person or to a ministry or the government.

Province: _____

District: _____

Division: _____   Date: _____

Village Name: _____   Time Start: _____   a.m./p.m.

Farmer's Name: _____   Finish: _____   a.m./p.m.

Village No. _____   Interviewer: _____

Farmer No. _____

Instructions

1.   Whenever unable to obtain an answer from a respondent, mark against that question: *DK* for Don't Know; *RA* for Refused to Answer; *NA* for Not Applicable. For RA and NA note reason.

2.   Probe for further answers and record extra notes whenever necessary. But be sure the answers are the respondent's. Do not try to help the farmer when he or she is answering the question.

3.   If a respondent understands the question, record this exact answer no matter how "wrong" or "silly" it might seem to you.

Questions
1.   Have you ever lived away from this village for a year or more?
☐ (0) No
☐ (1) Yes. If yes, ask: Where did you live?

☐ (2) In another village in which
District:

☐ (3) In a city in:

☐ (9) Other (specify)

2.   Have you learned a trade?
☐ (0) No
☐ (1) Yes. If yes, ask: What trade?
☐ (2) Tailoring
☐ (3) Wood carving
☐ (4) Weaving
☐ (5) Joining/Masonry
☐ (9) Other (specify):

3a.   Last year, did you earn money from occupations, work, or activities other than farming?

☐ (0) No
☐ (1) Yes. If yes, ask: What kind?
☐ (2) Tailoring
☐ (3) Carpentry
☐ (4) Laborer
☐ (5) Trading
☐ (9) Other (specify):

3b.   Is this work for
☐ (0) Wages/Salary
☐ (1) Self—employment?
☐ (2) Combinations of wages and self employment?

3c.   Which work earns the most money?
☐ (0) Farming
☐ (1) Other work
☐ (2) About the same

154

3d.   Which work takes the most of your time?
        ☐ (0) Other work
        ☐ (1) Farming
        ☐ (2) About the same

3e.   How do you generally spend your time when you are not working on your farm or for money?
        ☐ (0) Building construction and household repairs
        ☐ (1) Resting or visiting friends and relatives
        ☐ (9) Other (specify) _____

3f.   Do these non—farm activities (of the last question) take more or less of your time now than before the last ten years?

        ☐ (0) More
        ☐ (1) Less
        ☐ (2) About the same

4a.   How many children do you have living with you in your compound?
        No: _____

4b.   How many wives do you have? Total: _____
        (i)   Living in the same village? No: _____
        (ii)   Living elsewhere (second house)? No: _____

4c.   How many people other than your wives and children do you have living in your compound?

        No: _____

5.   How many people actually work for you on your farm?
        No: _____

5a.   How many months did *each group* work for you last year?
        (i.)   Children under 15 years.
                No.   Months: _____
        (ii.)   Children 15 years or older.
                No.   Months: _____
        (iii.) Wives.
                No.   Months: _____
        (iv.)   Relatives.
                No.   Months: _____
        (v.)   Permanent laborers.
                No.   Months: _____

(vi.) Laborers at busy time.
No.   Months: _____

6. Please tell me how and when you use hired labor.
(i.) In what months?

_____

(ii.) On what crops?

_____

(iii.) Where did you go to find laborers when you need some?

_____

(iv.) Where do most of your laborers come from?

Place: _____ Distance   from
here:_____

7. Please tell me about your farm lands.
(i.) How many farm plots do you have? No. _____

7a. For each farm, ask:
(i.) How far is that farm from the compound (nearest mile)?
_____

(ii.) How big is that farm?
(No. heaps or No. trees) _____

7b. What crops did you grow on that farm last year?

Plots	Distance	Size	Crops Grown
(i.)			
(ii.)			
(iii.)			
(iv.)			
(v.)			
(vi.)			

8.   What crops did you (or your wives) grow/harvest last year? For crops grown, which part of each crop was sold?

Crop	Not Grown or Harvested 0	Grown or Harvested 1	Not Sold 2	Less than Half Sold 3	More than Half Sold 4	All Sold 5
(i.) Coffee	☐	☐	☐	☐	☐	☐
(ii.) Tea	☐	☐	☐	☐	☐	☐
(iii.) Maize	☐	☐	☐	☐	☐	☐
(iv.) Horticulture	☐	☐	☐	☐	☐	☐
(v.) Beans	☐	☐	☐	☐	☐	☐
(vi.) Milk	☐	☐	☐	☐	☐	☐
(vii.) Sugar Cane	☐	☐	☐	☐	☐	☐
(viii. Pyrethrum	☐	☐	☐	☐	☐	☐
(ix.) Rice	☐	☐	☐	☐	☐	☐
(x.) Millet	☐	☐	☐	☐	☐	☐
(xi.) Sorghum	☐	☐	☐	☐	☐	☐
(xii. Potatoes	☐	☐	☐	☐	☐	☐
(xiii. Wheat	☐	☐	☐	☐	☐	☐
(xiv. Fruit	☐	☐	☐	☐	☐	☐

9a.   What do you consider to be the most important crops on your farm?
☐ (0) Maize
☐ (1) Coffee
☐ (2) Tea
☐ (3) Millet/Sorghum
☐ (4) Beans
☐ (5) Fruits
☐ (9) Other (specify) _____

9b.   Where do you sell these two crops?
☐ (0) In this village
☐ (1) On the roadside
☐ (2) In another village
☐ (3) In town

☐ (4) To a cooperative

10. Why didn't you plant more of the following crops this year?

Crop	No Need	All I could Maintain	Insufficient Labor	Land Shortage	Insufficient Capital	Uncertain Market	Prices Too Low	Other (Specify)
	0	1	2	3	4	5	6	9
(i.) Coffee	☐	☐	☐	☐	☐	☐	☐	_____
(ii.) Tea	☐	☐	☐	☐	☐	☐	☐	_____
(iii. Maize	☐	☐	☐	☐	☐	☐	☐	_____
(iv. Vegetables	☐	☐	☐	☐	☐	☐	☐	_____
(v.) Horticulture	☐	☐	☐	☐	☐	☐	☐	_____
(vi. Beans	☐	☐	☐	☐	☐	☐	☐	_____
(vii Pyrethrum	☐	☐	☐	☐	☐	☐	☐	_____
(vii Millet	☐	☐	☐	☐	☐	☐	☐	_____

11a. Do you grow both coffee/tea/pyrethrum and food crops?
☐ (0) No
☐ (1) Yes
☐ (9) If yes, which? _____

11b. Why do you grow both crops instead of only one?
☐ (0) To provide food for the family
☐ (1) To make money
☐ (9) Other (specify) _____

11c. What is your most important crop?
☐ (0) Coffee
☐ (1) Tea
☐ (2) Pyrethrum
☐ (3) Potatoes
☐ (4) Maize
☐ (5) Millet/Sorghum
☐ (9) Other (specify) _____

11d.   Why did you decide to grow that crop?
☐ (0) To provide food for the family
☐ (1) To make more money
☐ (2) Because export crops are permanent
☐ (9) Other (specify)   _____

12.   Suppose the government says that the prices of export crops will go up by 50% next year. Which of the following will you do?

☐ (0) Work harder on export crops and less on food crops
☐ (1) Work harder on both export crops and food crops
☐ (2) Work the same amount on export and food crops as before the price increase
☐ (9) Other (specify)   _____

13.   If the higher export price mentioned above were to be maintained for several years (say 3 to 5 years), which of the following would you do?

☐ (0) Work harder on export and less on food
☐ (1) Work harder on both export and food
☐ (2) Work the same amount on export and food as before
☐ (9) Other (specify)   _____

14.   Suppose the government says that the price of food crops will increase next while the price of export crops will remain the same. Which of the following would you do?

☐ (0) Work harder on food and less on exports
☐ (1) Work harder on both food and export crops
☐ (2) Work the same amount on food and exports as before the price increase
☐ (9) Other (specify)   _____

15.   If the higher food prices mentioned above were to be maintained for several years (3 to 5 years), which of the following would you do?

☐ (0) Work harder on food crops and less on export crops
☐ (1) Work harder on both export and food crops
☐ (2) Work the same amount on export and food crops as before
☐ (9) Other (specify)   _____

16. Suppose the prices of exports and the prices of food crops were to go up next year, which of the following would you do?
    ☐ (0) Work harder on exports and less on food crops
    ☐ (1) Work harder on both exports and food crops
    ☐ (2) Work less on both exports and food crops
    ☐ (3) Work the same amount on exports and food as before
    ☐ (9) Other (specify) _____

17. Compared with last year's price, the prices of export crops this year
    ☐ (0) Higher
    ☐ (1) Lower
    ☐ (2) About the same

18. What did you do as a result of the change in the price of exports from last year to this year?

    ☐ (0) Worked harder on exports and less on food crops
    ☐ (1) Worked harder on food crops and less on export crops
    ☐ (2) Work harder on both exports and food crops
    ☐ (3) Worked the same amount on both crops as last year
    ☐ (9) Other (specify) _____

19a. What are the major food crops eaten in this village?
    ☐ (0) Maize
    ☐ (1) Beans/vegetables
    ☐ (2) Potatoes
    ☐ (3) Cassava
    ☐ (4) Millet/Sorghum

19b. What kinds of food did most people eat in this village before maize became so important?

    1.
    2. _____
    3. _____
    4. _____
    5. _____
    6. _____
    7. _____
    8. _____

Bibliography

Abbot, P.C., and R.L. Thompson. "Changing Comparative Advantage." *Agricultural Economics (* 1987): 97—112.

Adelman, I., and C. T. Morris. *Economic Growth and Social Equity in Developing Countries*. California: Stanford University Press, 1973.

Ahluwalia, Montek S. "Rural poverty and agricultural performance in India." *Journal of development Studies* 14 (1978a): 298—32.

Ander, K. *Economic Growth, Comparative Advantage, and Agricultural Trade of Pacific Basin* (ed.) G .Edward Schuh and Jennifer L. McCoy. Boulder: Westview Press, 1986.

Askari, H., and J. T. Cummings. *Agricultural Supply Response: A Survey of the Econometric Evidence*. Washington: Preager, 1976.

Atkinson, A.B. "On measurement of inequality." *Journal of Economic Theory* (1970): 244—263.

Baker, D.C., and C.K. Eicher. "Agricultural Technology in Sub—Saharan Africa: A Critical Assessment." Paper presented at the 25th Annual Meeting of the African Studies Association, Washington, D.C., 1979.

Baker, D.C., and C.K. Eicher. "A Stages Approach to Comparative Advantage. In Economic Growth and Resources." Vol. 4. *National and International Issues*, (ed.) I. Adelman. New York: St.Martin's, 1982.

Bardhan, P.K. *Land, Labor and Rural Poverty*. Cambridge: Cambridge University, 1984.

Bardhan, P.K. *Interlocking factor markets and agrarian development*. A review of issues: Oxford Economic papers, 1980.

Bates, R.H. *Markets and states in tropical Africa: The political basis of agricultural policies*. Berkeley: University of California Press, 1981.

Bechu, N. 1998. "The Impact of AIDS on the Economy of Families in Cote d'Ivoire", from *Confronting AIDS: Evidence From The Developing World, Selected Background Papers for the World Bank Policy Research Report*, M. Ainsworth, L. Fransen, and M. Over, eds., European Commission: United Kingdom and Aids Analysis Africa, 8(1):2—3

Beneria, L. "Reproduction, Production and Sexual Division of Labor." *Cambridge Journal of Economics* (1977).

Berry, R.A., and W.R. Cline. *Agrarian structure and productivity in Developing Countries*. Baltimore: Johns Hopkins, 1979.

Berg, E.J. "Economies: The African Case." *Quarterly Journal of Economics* (1975).

Balasa, B. "Trade policies in developing countries." *American Economic Review* (1980).

Balasa, B. *Comparative Advantage Trade Policy and Economic Development*. New York: New York University Press, 1989.

Biggs, S.D. "A Multiple Source of Innovation Model of Agricultural Research and Technology Promotion." *World Development* 18 (1990).

Blanchard, F. "Demographic Pincer Closing on Industrialized World." *ILO Information* 15 (1979).

Boserup, E. *Women's Role in Economic Development*. London: George Allen Unwin, 1970.

Bryson, Judy C. "Women and Agriculture in Sub—Saharan Africa: Implications for Development (An Explanatory Study)." *Journal of Development Studies* 17 (1981).

Chichilinsky, G. "Terms of trade and domestic distribution: Export—led growth with abundant labor." *Journal of Development Economics* (1981): 163—192.

Clayton, E.S. *Agriculture, Poverty and Freedom in Developing Countries*. London: Macmillan, 1983.

Collier, P., and L. Deepak. "Poverty and growth in Kenya." *World Bank Staff Working Paper No.389*. Washington: World Bank, 1980.

Central Bureau of Statistics. *Proceedings on the workshop on Consumer price index and urban Household Budget Survey*. Nairobi: Government Printer, 1991.

Crawford, E. and E. Thorbecke. "Employment, Income Distribution, Poverty alleviation and Basic needs in Kenya." *Report of an ILO Consulting Mission*. Ithaca: Cornell University, 1978.

Deere, C.D. "Rural Women Subsistence Production in the Capitalist Periphery."

Review of Radical Political Economics 8 (1976).

Deere, C.D. "The Agricultural Division of Labor by Sex: Myths, Facts and Contradictions in the Northern Peruvian Sierra." Paper presented at the Joint National Meeting of the Latin American Studies Association, Houston, Texas, 1978.

Demeke, M. The Potential Impact of HIV/ AIDS on the Rural Sector of Ethiopia. Unpublished manuscript, January, 1993

Edholm, F., O. Harris, and K. Young. "Conceptualizing Women." *Critique of Anthropology* 9/10 (1977): 101—130.

Ellis, F. "Agricultural Price Policy in Tanzania." *World Development* (1982).

Ellis, F. *Peasant Economics: Farm Households and Agrarian Development.* Cambridge: Cambridge University Press, 1988a.

Ellis, F. *Agricultural Pricing Policy in Africa.* London: Macmillan, 1988b.

Ellis, F. *Agricultural Policies in Developing Countries.* Cambridge: Cambridge University Press, 1992.

Eicher, C.K., and J.M. Staatz, eds. *Agricultural Development in the Third World.* Baltimore: Johns Hopkins, 1984.

Feder, A. "On exports and economic growth." *Journal of Development Economics* (1983): 59—73.

Fei, J., and G. Ranis. *Development of labor surplus economy: Theory and Policy.* Homewood, 1964.

Ghatak, and Ingersent. *Agriculture and Economic Development.* Baltimore: Johns Hopkins, 1984.

Griffin, K. *Land concentration and Rural Poverty.* London: Macmillan, 1976.

Griffin, K. *The political Economy of Agrarian Change.* London: Macmillan, 1979b.

Gulati, Leela. "Occupational Distribution of working women. An Inter—State Comparison. " *Economic and Political Weekly* (1975).

Ilinigumugabo, A. "The Economic Consequences of AIDS in Africa." *African Journal of Fertility, Sexuality and Reproductive Health* 1 (1996): 153—61.

ILO. *Employment, Income, and Equality: A Strategy for Increasing Productive Employment in Kenya.* Geneva: U.N, 1972.

Johnson, B.F. "Agriculture and structural transformation in developing countries: A survey of research." *Journal of Economic Literature* (1970): 369—404.

Johnson, B.F., and W.C. Clark. *Redesigning rural development: A Strategic Perspective*. Baltimore: Johns Hopkins, 1982.

Jorgenson, D.W. "The development of dual economy." *Economic Journal* (1961): 309—334.

Kakwani, N.C. "On a class of poverty measures." *Econometrica* (1980): 437—446.

Krishna, R. *Price and Technology Policies: In Agricultural Development in Third World*. (Eds.) C.K. Eicher and J.M Staatz. Baltimore: Johns Hopkins, 1990.

Kuznets, S. "Economic growth and income inequality." *American Economic Review* 45 (1955): 1—28.

Kuznets, Simon. *Modern economic growth: Rate structure and spread*. New Haven: Yale University, 1966.

Kwaramba, P (1997) "The Socio—Economic Impact of HIV/ AIDS on Communal Agricultural Systems in Zimbabwe", *Zimbabwe Farmers Union, Friedrich Ebert Stiftung Economic Advisory Project, Working Paper 19*, Harare, Zimbabwe

Lele, Uma. "The Design of Development: Lessons from Africa." Baltimore: Johns Hopkins, 1979.

Lele, Uma. "Tanzania: Phoenix or Icarus?" *In world Economic Growth*. San Francisco: Studies Institute for Contemporary, 1984.

Lele, Uma. "*Rural* Africa: Modernization, Equity, and Long —Term Development." *In Agricultural Development in the Third World*. (Eds.) C.K Eicher and J.M Staatz. Baltimore: Johns Hopkins University, 1984.

Lele, Uma. "Agricultural Growth, Terms of Trade and Poverty Alleviation in Sub—Saharan Africa." *In Mellor and Desai. Agricultural Change and Rural Poverty*. Baltimore: Johns Hopkins, 1985.

Lele, Uma. and John W. Mellor. "Technological change distributive bias and labor transfer in a two sector economy." *Oxford Economic Papers* (1981): 426—41.

Lewis, W. A. "Economic Development with Unlimited Supplies of Labor." *Manchester School*. Manchester: Manchester School Press, (1954): 139—191.

Lipton, M. "Farm Price Stabilization in Underdeveloped Agriculture: Some Effects on

Income Stability and Income Distribution." *In unfashionable Economics.* (eds) P.Streten. London: Weidenfeld & Nicholson, 1980.

Lloyd, C. *Sex, Discrimination and the Division of Labour.* New York: Columbia University Press, 1976.

Little, I.M., D.Scitovsky, and M. Scot. *Industry and trade in developing countries.* London: Oxford, 1970.

Little, I.M., D.Scitovsky, and M. Scot. *Economic development: Theory, Policy and international relations.* New York: Basic books, 1982.

Mars, T. and G. White. "Developmental states in African Agriculture." *IDS Bulletin* 17 (1986).

Mellor, John W. and Bruce Johnson. "The world food equation: Interrelations among development, employment, and food consumption." *Journal of Economic Literature* (1984).

Mellor, John W. "The use and productivity of farm family labor in early stages of agricultural development." *Journal of Farm Economics* (1963): 517—34.

Mellor, John W. "The functions of agricultural prices in economic development." *Indian Journal of Agricultural Economics* January—March (1968): 23—27.

Mellor, John W. " Food price policy and income distribution in low income countries." *Economic development and cultural change* (1978): 1—26.

Mellor, John W. and Uma Lele. "Growth linkage of the new food grain technologies." *Indian Journal of Agricultural Economics* 28 (1973).

Mennon, Wawer, Konde—Lule, Sewankabo, Li, 1998 "The Economic Impact of Adult Mortality on Households in Rakai District", from *Confronting AIDS: Evidence From the Developing World*, (eds) Ainsworth and Fransen, European Commission: United Kingdom

Mynt, H., *The classical theory of international trade and underdeveloped countries.* Oxford: Blackwell, 1958.

Moock, J.L. and B.N. Okigbo, eds. *Understanding Africa's Rural Households and Farming Systems.* Boulder: Homewood, 1986.

Narain, Dharm. "Growth of productivity in Indian agriculture." *Journal of Agricultural Economics* 32 (1976).

Narain, Dharm. *The dynamics of supply: Estimation of farmers response to price.* Baltimore: John Hopkins, 1958.

Nerlove, Marc. "The dynamics of supply: Retrospect and Prospect." *American Journal of Agricultural Economics* (1979): 496—509.

Newberry, D.M.G., and J.E. Stiglitz. *The theory of commodity price stabilization.* Oxford: Clarendon, 1981.

Over and Ainsworth, et. al. 1996, *Coping With AIDS: The Economic Impact of Adult Mortality from AIDS and Other Causes on Households in Kagera,* Tanzania

Prebisch, R. *The economic development of Latin America and its principal problems.* New York: U.N, 1950.

Rosenstein—Rodan, P.N. "Problems of industrialization of Eastern and South—Eastern Europe." *Economic Journal* June/September (1943): 202—211.

Ritson, C. "A framework for analyzing the contribution of agricultural sector to economic development." *Journal of Agricultural Economics* August (1973).

Sandbrook, R. "The State and Economic Stagnation in Tropical Africa." *World Development* (1986).

Scandizzo, P.I, and Bruce, C. "Methodology for Measuring Agricultural Price Intervention Effects." *World Bank Staff Paper No.394,* Washington, D.C.: World Bank, 1980.

Sen, Amartya K. "Peasant and dualism with or without surplus labor." *Journal of Political Economy* October (1966): 425—450.

Sen, Amartya K. "Levels of Poverty: Policy Change." *World Bank Staff Working Paper No.401,* Washington, D.C.: World Bank, 1980.

Sen, Amartya K. "Ingredients of famine analysis: Availability and entitlements." *Quarterly Journal of Economics* 96 (1981a): 433—64.

Shorrocks, A.F. "The class of decomposable Inequality Measures." *Econometrica* (1980): 613—625.

Stewart, F. *Macro—Policies for Appropriate Technology in Developing Countries.* Colorado: Westview Press, 1978.

Sukhatme, P.N. "Assessment of inadequacy of diets of different income levels." *Economic and Political Weekly* August (1978).

Stewart, Frances. *Technology and Underdevelopment*. London: Macmillan, 1978.

Stiglitz, J.E. *The Economics of Public Sector*. New York: Norton and Company, 1986a.

Stiglitz, J.E. "The New Development Economics." *World Development* (1986b).

Streeten, P. *What Price Food? Agricultural Price Policies in Developing Countries*. London: Macmillan, 1987.

Ndongko, Theresa. "Tradition and the role of women in Africa." *Presence Afracaine* (1976).

Thorbecke, E. and I. Hall, eds. *Agricultural Sector Analysis and Models in Developing Countries*. Rome: FAO, 1985.

Timmer, C.P., W.P. Falcon, and S.R. Pearson. *Food Policy Analysis*. Baltimore: Johns Hopkins, 1983.

Tolley, G.S., V. Thomas, and C.M. Wong. *Agricultural Price Policies and the Developing Countries*. Baltimore: Johns Hopkins,1982.

USDA. "Food Problems and prospects in Sub—Saharan Africa: The decade of 1980's." *Foreign Agricultural Economic Report 166*, Washington: D.C., 1981.

Westlake, M. J. "The Measurement of Agricultural Price Distortion in Developing Countries." *Journal of Development Studies* 23 (1987).

Taylor, Lance. *Global Macroeconomics*. New York: Basic Books, 1983.

Vanek, J. "Time Spent in Housework." *Scientific American* (1970): 116—20.

Wolgin, J.M. "Resource allocation and risk: a case study of small holder agriculture in Kenya." *American Journal of Agricultural Economics* (1980).

World Bank. *The Assault on World Poverty*. Baltimore: Johns Hopkins University Press, 1975, pp.187—261.

World Bank. *Kenya: Growth and Structural Change*. Washington: World Bank, 1983a.

World Bank. *Poverty and Hunger: Issues and Options for Food Security in Developing Countries*. Washington, D.C.: World Bank, 1986a.

World Bank. *World Development Report*. Washington: World Bank, 1975.

Wolpe, H, 1975,"The Theory of Colonialism: The South African Case" in oxaal, I., et al.

(eds.), *Beyond the sociology of Development*, London: Routledge, 1975.

Index

Endnotes

Chapter 1— Poverty

1 Hunt Diana, *The Impending Crises in Kenya*, London: Gower, 1986.
2 Collier, P., and L. Deepak. "Poverty and Growth in Kenya." *World Bank Staff Working Paper No.389*. Washington: World Bank, 1980.
3 Crawford, E and E. Thorbecke. "Employment, Income Distribution, Poverty Alleviation and Basic Needs in Kenya." *Report of an ILO Consulting Mission*. Ithaca: Cornell University, 1983.

Chapter 3 — Agriculture

4 Berry, R. A., and W.R. Cline. *Agrarian structure and productivity in Developing Countries*. Baltimore: John Hopkins, 1979; Ghatak,L and Ingersent *Agriculture and Economic Development*, Baltimore, John Hopkins, 1982 "and" Askari and *Cummings Agricultural Supply Response: A Survey of the Econometric Evidence*, (1976).
5 Note that, as we argued earlier, a shift in favor of food production due to an increase in the price of food is not likely to increase **F** and may diminish it.
6 The level of the farmer's real income need not affect the level of the "reservation demand" since it is no more than his insurance against starvation in bad years for export crop. On the other hand, it may vary with the size of the farmer's family assuming that he is much concerned with taking out "insurance" for his family as he is for himself. It is assumed that the farmer can produce at least this much food if he employed all his resources in food production and that on the farm.
7 This due to fluctuations in the weather conditions and each crop responds in a different way.
8 Biral Yesilada. "Agrarian Reform in Reverse. The Food Crisis in the Third World." *Westview Special Studies in Agricultural Sciences   and Policy*, 1987, pp.184.

Chapter 4 – Conceptualized Framework

ix In most theoretical models of LDCs, the relationship between sectoral rather than aggregate growth rates have received a great deal of attention from researchers and economists. It has been argued that while aggregate growth models as postulated by Harrod, Domar, Solow and Kaldor are useful, they don't address the dualistic nature of LDCs, whereby the market is imperfect and disguised unemployment renders marginal productivity impossible. See, Jones, R.W., "Presumption and the transfer problem." *Journal of International Economics*, 1976. pp.263—274.

x Lele Uma. "Terms of Trade, Agricultural Growth and Rural Poverty in Africa." Mellor and Desai, Eds. *Agricultural Change and Rural Poverty*,.Baltimore: Johns Hopkins University Press, 1985.

xi Note the signs of the coefficients of the linear model in influencing the dependent variable.

xii Ghatak and Ingersent. *Agriculture and Economic Development*. Baltimore: Johns Hopkins, 1984.

xiiiState intervention in development process has been recognized even recently by the World Bank Reports, but the idea goes back to the so called latecomers such as Germany, the United States, Japan, and most recently the New Industrializing Countries. In late eighteenth century and nineteenth century arguments in favor of state intervention were infant industry and infant nation arguments but currently being used to block competition.

xiv Woldesmate and Cox. "The Food Crisis in Kenya in Agrarian Reform in Reverse. The Food Crisis in the Third World." *Westview Special Studies in Agricultural Science and Policy*, 1987.

xv Boserup, E. *Women's Role in Economic Development*. London: Goerge Allen Unwin, 1970.

xvi Ndongko, Theresa. *Tradition and the role of women in Africa*. Paris: Presence Africaine, 1976, pp. 147.

xvii Lloyd , C. *Sex, Discrimination and the Division of Labor*. New York: Columbia University Press, 1976.

xviii Bryson, Judy C. "Women and Agriculture in Sub—Saharan Africa: Implications for Development (An Explanatory Study*)." Journal of Development Studies* 17 (1981).

xix Beneria, L. "Reproduction, Production and Sexual Division of Labor." *Cambridge Journal of Economics* (1977).

xx Blanchard, F. "Demographic Pincer Closing on Industrialized World." *ILO Information* 15 (1979).

xxi Deere, C.D. "Rural Women Subsistence Production in the Capitalist Periphery." *Review of Radical Political Economics* 8 (1976).

xxii Gulati,Leela. " Occupational Distribution of Working Women. An Inter—State Comparison." *Economic and Political Weekly* (1975).

xxiii Bryson , Judy C. "Women and Economic Development in Cameroon." *United States Agency for International Development*, 1976.

Chapter 5 – Impact of HIV/ Aids on Poverty

24 Mead Over, Martha Ainsworth, et al. 1996. Coping with AIDS: The Economic Impact of Adult Mortality from AIDS and Other Causes on Households in Kagera, Tanzania.

25 Bechu, N. 1998. "The impact of AIDS on the Economy of Families in Cote d'Ivoire," from *Confronting* Aids: *Evidence From The Developing World, Selected Background Papers for the World Bank Policy Research Report*, M. Ainsworth, L. Fransen, and M. Over, eds., European Commission: United Kingdom and Aids Analysis Africa 8(1):2—3

26 Mennon, R., M..J Wawer, J.K. Konde—Lule, N.K. Sewankambo, and C. Li. 1998. "The Economic Impact of Adult Mortality on Households in Rakai district", from *Confronting* AIDS: *Evidence from the Developing World,: (eds)* Ainsworth and Fransen, European Commission: United Kingdom

27 Demeke, M. The Potential Impact of HIV/AIDS on the Rural Sector of Ethiopia. Unpublished manuscript, 1993

28 Ilinigumugabo, A. "The Economic Consequences of AIDS in Africa." *African Journal of Fertility, Sexuality and Reproductive Health* 1 (1996):153—61.

29 Kwaramba, P "The Socio—Economic Impact of HIV/AIDS on Communal Agricultural Systems in Zimbabwe," Zimbabwe Farmers Union, Friedrich Ebert Stiftung Economic Advisory Project, *Working Paper 19*, Harare, Zimbabwe (1997).

30 Demeke, M. The Potential Impact of HIV/AIDS on the Rural Sector of Ethiopia. Unpublished manuscript, 1993.

31 Jones, C. 1997. What HIV cost a tea estate in Malawi. *AIDS Analysis Africa*; 7(3): 5—7.

32 Roberts, Matthew and Bill Rau, African Workplace Profiles: Private Sector AIDS Policy, *AIDSCAP*, Arlington, VA, USA.

33 : Roberts, Matthew and Bill Rau, African Workplace Profiles: Private Sector AIDS Policy, *AIDSCAP*, Arlington, VA, USA

34 Roberts, Matthew and Bill Rau, African Workplace Profiles: Private Sector AIDS Policy, *AIDSCAP*, Arlington, VA, USA.; Aventin, L and P Huard. 1997. HIV/AIDS and manufacturing in Abidjan. *AIDS Analysis Africa*, Vol 7(3): June 1997.; Ainsworth, Martha, "The Impact of HIV/AIDS on African Development", presented at the African Development Bank HIV/AIDS and Development in Africa Symposium, May 11, 1993.

35 *Southern African Economist*, 1997. "AIDS toll on regional economies," April 15—May 15, 1997.

36 *Southern African Economist*, 1997. "AIDS toll on regional economies," April 15—May 15, 1997.

37 Ainsworth, Martha, "The Impact of HIV/AIDS on African Development", presented at the African Development Bank HIV/AIDS and Development in Africa Symposium, May 11, 1993.

38 *Southern African Economist*, 1997. "AIDS toll on regional economies," April 15—May 15, 1997.

39 Ministry of Health, 1998. *AIDS in Ethiopia, Second Edition*, Addis Ababa: Epidemiology and AIDS Department, 1998.; NASCOP, 1998. *AIDS in Kenya, Fourth Edition*. Nairobi: National AIDS and STDs Control Programme, 1998.; Ministry of Health and Child Welfare, 1998. *HIV/AIDS in Zimbabwe*. Harare: National AIDS Coordination Programme, 1998.

40 *AIDS Analysis Africa*, Vol. 4 (5), September/October 1994.

41 UNAIDS, 1998. *Report on the global HIV/AIDS epidemic, June 1998*. Geneva: UNAIDS, WHO,. 1998.

42 Over, Mead, 1992. "The Macroeconomic impact of AIDS in Sub—Saharan Africa," The World Bank, *Technical Working Paper No. 3.*, 1992.

43 Kambou, Gerard, Shantayanan Deverajan and Mead Over. 1992. "The Economic Impact of AIDS in an African Country: Simulations with a Computable General Equilibrium Model of Cameroon", *Journal of African Economies*, Volume 1, Number 1.

44 Forgy, Larry. 1993. "Mitigating AIDS: The Economic Impacts of AIDS inZambia and Measures to Counter Them," *REDSO/ESA*, February 1993.

45 Cuddington, JT, 1992. Modelling the Macroeconomic Effects of AIDS, with an Application to Tanzania, *World Bank Economic Review*, 7(2):172—189.

46 Hancock, John; David Nalo; Monica Aoko; Roselyn Mutemi; Steven Forsythe, 1996. "The Macroeconomic Impacts of AIDS," *AIDS in Kenya*, FHI: Washington, DC, 1996.

47 World Bank, 1997. *Confronting AIDS: Public Priorities in a Global Epidemic*. New York: Oxford University Press.